Mustang

Sharing My Story of ADHD, Imposter Syndrome, and Resilience

Sharon "Shay" Jordan

Ellasal Press

Mustang

Sharing My Story of ADHD, Imposter Syndrome, and Resilience

Sharon "Shay" Jordan

FIRST PRINTING

ISBN: 979-8-9881841-0-2

eBook ISBN: 979-8-9881841-1-9

Hardcover: 979-8-9881841-2-6

Library of Congress Control Number: 2023906971

ELLASAL PRESS

To:

Daddy, I love you. You were always there for me. Always.

Muh, for sharing God's light on me. Truly you raised me so that I would not depart from Jesus Christ.

Mama, As I wrote this book, I realized that you were (or we both were) naive to my disease, but your tough love molded me into the mustang that I became, branding me with the toughness I would need to survive. I love you. Rest in peace.

The women in my life who inspired me to keep it moving forward.

My troops on the LaSalle, I'm most grateful to have had the ability to lead and train you, regardless of my personal struggles. I'm no prouder of anything else in my life. I served with the finest who, in turn, made me the finest.

The leaders I was blessed to have, from bootcamp to CWO, guiding me, encouraging me, keeping me on course, and seeing in me what I could never see.

To my true friends. You know who you are.

FOREWORD

I have known Sharon (Shay) Jordan for over thirty years. We were first introduced walking through a crossover passageway while I was assigned to the Bureau of Naval Personnel in Washington, DC. At that time in her military career, she was a hard-charging, energetic Chief Petty Officer who was always looking for ways to accelerate her career. She had been an outspoken woman who had not been willing to compromise her principles with juniors, seniors, or peers.

I am not surprised she had the courage to put her life's adventures into writing and share them with little to no transparency. Shay Jordan is a role model for all little girls, teenagers, and young adult women in the twenty-first century. She has been one who has known her worth and set her sail to accomplish it all. In this book, she speaks of the challenges and struggles that she's endured and overcome, by, I strongly believe, her faith in God, instilled by her grandmother.

I would invite all who pick up this book to read it with a fresh belief that all things are possible regardless of who you are or whatever situation in life you may find yourself in. All of us cannot have the resounding name and stature of a Betty Shabazz, Coretta Scott King, Justice Ketanji Brown Jackson, Maya Angelou, or Michelle Obama, but our stories and lives can and do speak great volumes and do impact the world. Many lives have been changed and redirected because people encountered Sharon "Shay" Jordan on their journeys of life.

The opportunity to write this foreword has been a great honor and privilege for me to say something on behalf of my eternal friend and shipmate Chief Warrant Officer Sharon "Shay" Jordan.

Dr. Drexel N. Mitchell, Sr.
(Master Chief Petty Officer, U. S. Navy, Retired)

Wherefore take unto you the whole armour of God, that ye may be able to withstand in the evil day, and having done all, to stand.

—Ephesians 6:13

Chapter 1

Diagnosis

I had been retired for three years. It had been the right time to retire, but that didn't mean that retirement necessarily agreed with me. I found myself feeling anxious and depressed much of the time. Worse, I found myself struggling to focus. I'd even had a couple of minor car accidents, consequences of not paying attention or simply reacting too slowly.

This inability to focus wasn't exactly new. Neither were the depression and anxiety. Maybe it was just more noticeable now. In fact, I'd had problems since childhood. During my military years, I guess I didn't have time to be preoccupied with emotional issues. Now there was more free time. But free time wasn't really free. In retirement, my emotional issues seemed to come at me with a vengeance.

I talked to my primary care physician at the VA Medical Center in Louisville, Kentucky who suggested some tests. A psychological assessment. The results indicated I had dysthymic depression, otherwise known as persistent depressive disorder. The tests further indicated that I had unspecified anxiety, which is pretty much what it sounds like. I was restless, couldn't sleep, fearful—and all of it with no apparent reason behind it.

I did a fair amount of internet research and repeatedly came across another disorder that seemed, to me, even more fitting. Two years after the first assessment, I got another one, this one more comprehensive than the first. This one included more detailed interviews, the filling out of extensive questionnaires, and tests that measured memory and cognitive abilities. Dr. Melissa Boyles, a neuropsychologist at the center, came back with a different diagnosis this time: Attention Deficit Hyperactivity Disorder—ADHD.

The diagnosis did not surprise me. It was, in fact, the disorder I had read about online. Strangely, the diagnosis was something of a relief. There was a name for what I had. I wasn't crazy. I was not alone. My issues were real and no longer "unspecified."

Further, the diagnosis explained a lot of what I had experienced from a very early age. Although I was just now discovering what I had, ADHD was something I'd suffered with for as long as I could remember. And it made me wonder how I'd done it. How I'd managed to not just survive in my career, but thrive in it. Where did the strength come from? And how in God's name did I manage to focus?

It's funny looking back, but I didn't see myself thriving at the time. I didn't see the focus. I didn't grasp the success, yet it's clear by any objective standard—and the military is big on objective standards—that I made something of myself, even if I couldn't see it happening or understand how I was doing it.

Chapter 2

April Fool's Day

Yep, it was April Fool's Day, but it sure didn't appear that way to me. I'd never been more serious about anything in my life. It was only the second time I'd ever been on an airplane, which always seemed to me such a glamorous way to travel. But I was excited by more than just the mode of transportation. I was excited about where I was going.

And I was excited about leaving.

I wasn't likely to miss my manager at Walgreens, that was for sure. A white woman, she seemed to have had it in for me from the day I started working there. Maybe it was racism, although, at the age of eighteen, I was probably too naïve to see it as that. Or maybe I had an idea that it was racism, but what could I have done about it? Either way, the woman seemed to relish the power she had over me. She might have even known about the Kroger incident, which probably wouldn't have helped her opinion of me.

The Kroger incident was stupid, I admit. But I was a kid and I'd never done anything like it before in my life. I had gone to work at Kroger the year before, shortly after high school graduation. My mother would work for the Kroger grocery chain for thirty-three years and it was she who got me the job as a cashier. She wanted me to stay busy and out of the house. "You gonna go to work or you gonna go to college," she said, "but you gettin' out of here." She got my two brothers jobs at Kroger, too. An uncle worked for Kroger and so did my two nephews.

Mama worked at a Kroger in the west end of Louisville. I went to work at Kroger in the southeastern part. It was a boy who got me into trouble. You could hardly call him a boyfriend, but I guess I liked Rasheeno enough, and when he and his buddy Maurice said they were going to be having a party and wanted a little help with the beer and snacks, I said, sure, I'll hook you up.

I still don't know how they spotted me, first, ringing up the Pabst Blue Ribbon that Rasheeno and Maurice had brought to my checkout lane and, second, taking it right off. These were the early days of scanners and I thought I was doing it right. Scan it, take it off. Bag it, print the receipt. Total: $0.00. The cashier's booth at the front of the store provided an overview of the registers, so maybe someone in there had spied on me. Or maybe someone tipped them off. Or maybe the manager had dealt with Rasheeno before. That might explain why the police were waiting for him and Maurice just outside the store. Not long after that, I saw a security guard walking toward me and I knew I was busted.

They escorted me up to the office and for a moment I hoped that being Mary Lillie Rucker's daughter might pay off. Mama was a loyal employee and a well-liked person. Everyone loved Mary Lillie, or "Marelilly," the way people said her name. She enjoyed a good time and was genuinely nice to everybody—me, at times, being the exception. But instead of cutting me a break, they took me to jail. On the way out, I called a girlfriend of mine and told her to call my mother to let her know what happened. *I* wasn't going to tell her.

I was sorry I had let my mother down, but just as sorry that I'd let my grandmother down. After all, it seemed as if I was always letting Mama down in one way or another. My grandmother, on the other hand, had been my rock, the single most influential person of my young life, dragging me to church every Sunday and Bible study every Wednesday. She was, perhaps, my lone role model. But even with my grandmother, the advice was always the same: "Pray on it." We called my grandmother "Mother," typically pronounced "Mutha," or shortened to "Muh." Muh's advice, short as it was, was normally better than Mama's advice, which was usually something along the lines of, "You need to comb that head of yours," or "Clean up that messy room!"

There was very little I could do that would satisfy Mama. Sometimes, I felt unwelcomed in my own home, like I was in the wrong place. I stayed in my room a great deal or else hung out in the basement. Mama had a knack for making me feel like less than I was. With a perpetual smirk, she'd convey to me that, no matter what it was, I was never going to get it right.

For more tangible direction and support, there was always Mr. and Mrs. Clark who lived across the street, a very kind couple. Mr. Clark was just a little too kind to young girls, however. I had no idea at the time that he was a pedophile, nor what a pedophile even was. But I loved Mrs. Clark. She was interested in my well-being and was always asking how I was getting along and what I was planning to do, showing interest in me that Mama rarely showed.

At the department of corrections downtown, they gave me one phone call. *I don't know what good this is gonna do*, I thought, but called home anyway. My brother Jerry answered and I could hear Mama, who'd already heard the news by then from her Kroger colleagues, in the background. "Leave her there," she was saying. "Just leave her in there." Maybe it was tough love, but this statement wounded me, more than I could know at the time, and haunt me well into adulthood.

Jerry said not to worry. "Me and Daddy'll come down to get you." My parents had divorced years before, but Daddy still came around from time to time. Years later, Mrs. Clark would tell me of how my mother resented my relationship with Daddy.

Sure enough, Rasheeno and Maurice were prior offenders and had to go in front of a grand jury and that's pretty much where I lost track of them. As for me, Mama's attorney, the one she used for her divorce, asked that I be put in the state's diversion program. This was for first-timers, a way to rehabilitate yourself before you ended up in a life of crime. The diversion program entailed a meeting downtown every other week with a caseworker, who asked me lots of questions about what I was doing and who I was hanging out with. Her office was in the same place where all the parolees went to meet their parole officers and I couldn't help but feel as though I'd been thrown into the same category as hardened criminals even though my crime was for a cart of snacks and cheap beer that added up to just over a hundred bucks. I began to resent the meetings and I didn't exactly treat the caseworker kindly. Then again, her responses to me were equally rude and in retrospect, I'm not sure she was a person who cared very much for her job.

My real contrition for my crime came in church. "You've made a mistake," said Mother, "and you need to move forward, starting with going to church and asking God for forgiveness." My grandmother, in typical form, was prayerful about the matter, and sympathetic. I didn't get much sympathy from Mama. Then again, I didn't feel as though I deserved it, either.

In church, I did better than ask God for forgiveness. One Sunday, full of jitters and alone, I stood before the congregation and confessed my crime. Mama was behind me in the choir, Mother was in the front pew. "I done wrong," I said. "I let my grandmother and mother down and I ask for God's forgiveness and the church's forgiveness, and for my mother and grandmother to forgive me." Mother came up and stood with me after I spoke. Mama remained seated where she was. Confessing to the whole church was the hardest thing I had ever done but I felt as if I needed to do it, telling myself to tough it out and get through it. It wouldn't be the last time I'd have to tough it out in life.

I tried college after Kroger, but ended up dropping out of the University of Louisville. I wasn't a bad student and, in fact, I was pretty good in English. I liked to write and kept a journal since tenth grade. My English professor encouraged me to continue writing and I haven't stopped since. It helps me focus, something I've struggled with my whole life, only discovering why relatively recently. But outside of writing, school held little interest for me. I didn't know what I wanted to do, but I knew I didn't want to learn anymore, at least not then.

And so there I was at Walgreens. Clearly, my future prospects weren't exactly what you'd call dazzling. I wasn't feeling school very much and I had no real marketable skills. Friends of mine were having babies. A couple of them already had them by the ages of fifteen or sixteen, but I surely didn't want that either.

I'd hit a dead end. And I was confused. On some level, I knew it was probably normal to be confused at the age of eighteen, but I also knew that eventually, I was going to have to figure out my path. I had to think about my future.

There was only one thing that held any sort of appeal for me, one thing that seemed like it possessed any kind of potential. It came from those TV ads: uniformed men and women doing exciting things in exotic places all over the world. "Be all you can be," the Army ads would say. The Navy promised that "It's not just a job, it's an adventure!" The Marines talked about "The Few, the Proud." And they all promised they'd help with continuing education. I remembered the ROTC kids in high school, marching down the hallways with their sharp-looking dress uniforms. Military service. That was the life for me.

I tried the Air Force first. Those ads were the most glamorous of all, with fighter jets screaming against the sky or taking off from aircraft carriers. I took the entrance exam, a mix of general knowledge questions—math, science, English, and the like, and came up two points shy of the required score. "Come back and take the test again," the recruiter told me. I spent a couple of weeks studying and went back to the recruitment office ready to give the test another try but the recruiter was out that day. So, lucky me, the Navy recruitment office was right across the hall. An opportunistic Navy recruiter—Petty Officer First Class Tyrone Wilson—saw me and invited me in.

"You know, it might be a while before the Air Force guy comes back," said Petty Officer Wilson. "But while you're here, why don't I go ahead and tell you what *we* can do for you?" And that's how I chose the Navy. Or, rather, how the Navy chose me. I took the oath and, for the first time in my life, I felt a purpose.

I solemnly swear that I will support and defend the Constitution of the United States against all enemies, foreign and domestic; that I will bear true faith and allegiance to the same; and that I will obey the orders of the President of the United States and the orders of the officers appointed over me, according to regulations and the Uniform Code of Military Justice. So help me God.

At home, everyone was more or less happy for me, although Mama wondered aloud why I would want to do something like join the Navy. Eventually, she'd be supportive in her own way; I knew she'd pray for me. But there was a twinge of guilt I felt, too. I had a constant hold on myself to be there for Mama. It seemed as if there was always something that she needed from me. In what had been, and would continue to be, an ongoing theme in my life, I felt an inordinate amount of responsibility for the family, as though it was my role to make everything work. How could I do that if I was away serving my country? But that same pressing feeling is also what drove me to seek more independence from my family.

Meanwhile, it was November and the Navy couldn't take me for a few months, so I enlisted on delayed entry, working at the Walgreens until I just couldn't take it anymore. I'd been getting enough grief from Mama at home and all I'd wanted to do was work in peace. I don't remember the final straw, but I vividly remember turning to the manager and saying, "You know what? I'm done." And I walked out the door.

And then before I knew it, it was the first of April and I was flying to Orlando to the Naval Training Center, knowing there was so much more for me where I was going, so much more than what I'd had in Louisville, or would ever have. I was ready now to begin my life. I was flying toward my future and leaving Louisville—leaving my childhood—behind.

CHAPTER 3

MAMA AND MOTHER

I was two when Mama and Mother went in together and bought a house. This effectively represented the end of my parents' marriage even though the divorce wouldn't be finalized for several more years. I can't say what led to the breakup. Was my dad cheating on Mama? Daddy, John Wesley Rucker, nicknamed Jayhawk by his buddies, was handsome and I'm willing to bet he fell into temptation. Then again, Mama's old pics reveal that she was a real piece of eye-candy. I'm certain they were an attractive couple when they were younger. He was born in 1928 and she in 1930.

They met at Central High School where Daddy played football and after they were married they lived on Jacob Street in an area of town known as the Bottoms. Later, I would learn that this was a term used in a lot of cities to describe the Black, segregated part of town. There were social clubs and juke joints and my parents not only lived in the Bottoms, but did a lot of partying and hanging out there. Both enjoyed a good time.

Whether Daddy cheated or whether it was his drinking or whether it was both, when they separated, Daddy somehow managed to work his way back in, at least enough to where he could drop by on occasion and have a couple of "smiles" in the kitchen, which is what he called his Falls City beers or his half-pints of Wild Irish Rose. But by the time of the divorce, he wasn't coming around much at all, especially when he knew Mama was at home. Daddy always walked everywhere and often times, he'd walk up 35th Street, which ran by the side of our house. I would hang out on the porch in hopes he'd come by. He'd give me a hug and say, "Hey, baby girl." Then he'd always ask, "Where's your mama?" With a teasing grin, he'd add, "Tell her I love her and tell her, 'Darling, without you I can't go on for your love means too much to me.'" With his hand over his heart, he'd say the same thing every time I'd see him and I would always laugh. He said it jokingly, but I can now see there was more than a hint of truth behind it. The divorce was clearly Mama's idea. Whatever it was that Daddy did to deserve getting kicked out, he regretted it. He carried on like it hadn't affected him, but years later he would write to me and tell me how crushed he had been. "I was a fool," he wrote.

Mama was working for Kroger by the time she and Mother bought the house together. She'd received a certificate in accounting but had chosen not to pursue a degree after high school. She was always good with numbers and I remember her drilling me on my times tables. At the Kroger, she was so fast on the cash register that everyone lined up at her checkout lane. Whether my grandmother didn't have the money to send her to school, or whether Mama just lost interest, I can't say. When I joined the Navy, I gravitated toward accounting, too, thinking I could be swift with numbers just like Mama. But I didn't have the patience or discipline to be able to finesse numbers as skillfully and I'd end up going in another direction.

Other than my grandmother, I knew practically nothing about my grandparents. Mother had four children with three daddies. Mama's dad never came around. In fact, Mama would try to meet him one day, going to his house, but he refused to come to the door. Apparently, to others, he would say that he had no daughter, which I can imagine was heartbreaking for Mama to hear. My paternal grandparents were named Charles and Mary, and that's about all I know about them other than the fact that they were mulatto. My father was raised mostly by his grandmother. In our house, it was Mother, Mama, my Aunt Sandra and her daughter Stephanie (both of whom eventually moved out), and my older brother Ricky who was born about four years before me. Jerry, my oldest brother, was out of the house by then. My grandmother had a brother named Wesley who lived with us for a little while after relocating from New York. He was well-spoken and always dressed sharp. He played classical piano and later, I would learn he was gay. One day, I learned he had a wooden leg. I accidentally caught him strapping it on one time. I'm sure my eyes must have gotten huge, and I thought, *wow, all along I just thought he had a bad hip!*

Another brother of Mother's was my Uncle Sam, who would drop by with his wife Mattie. Uncle Sam stayed drunk and Aunt Mattie had but one tooth in her head. Mother's two sons—my Uncle Henry, whom everyone called "Snookum," and Uncle Pete—would come by for Thanksgivings and Christmases with their families and the house was always loud and full during the holidays, kids playing out in the yard and in the basement, and grown folk in the living room or in the kitchen playing cards.

In the home, it was my grandmother who assumed the role of mother to all of us, and so it was no coincidence that we all called her that. Besides taking us to church and Bible study, Mother did most of the cooking, although it was pretty basic fare—pork chops, chicken, mashed potatoes, peas. In addition, she made us do our chores, pressed our hair, and was the disciplinarian of the household, although Mama didn't let her monopolize that last one. Mama wasn't shy about breaking out the extension cord for a good whippin' if I came home after the street lights came on, or if she got an early and unfavorable news report in her checkout lane at the Kroger from one of her top spies from my school. But a lot of evenings, Mama was out. She'd come home from a day of work, change her clothes, and leave again. Sometimes when she'd come home later that night, she'd wake me and say, "Sharon, get up and clean that kitchen. You know better." Her way of saying I'd done a half-assed job of cleaning the kitchen earlier that evening. In fact, Mama was in the habit of leaving me a list of chores to be done every day. And I knew they'd better all be done by the time she got home, and they'd better be done right.

For the most part, however, the majority of my instructions came from Mother. She taught me how to sew and cook and made me memorize the books of the Bible. One Easter Sunday, she made me sing "He Lives" in front of everybody. As far as my schooling, outside of those multiplication table drills, I can't think of a whole lot of involvement Mama had. Thinking back in naval terms, I guess Mother was my leading petty officer in charge while Mama was my chief.

Stephanie and I grew up like sisters and we played together all the time, even after Aunt Sandra got them a place of their own. Sandra would frequently drop

Stephanie off at our house on her way to work, often for whole weekends. We'd hang out in the basement and have our own little talent shows, singing pop music and gospel. But as I grew a little older, I found myself spending more and more time out of the house, mostly at my friend Kim's house one street over. Her mother—Miss Barbara—became like a second mom to me. She was like a second mother to a lot of kids in the neighborhood. Sometimes I'd hang around with her even when Kim wasn't around. Miss Barbara could make anyone feel special, something many of us kids, me especially, needed a lot more of.

The same could be said for Miss Bailey, who lived across the street. I was friends with her daughter Lisa, and, just like with Miss Barbara, I sometimes spent time with Miss Bailey even when her daughter wasn't home. Lisa was a voluptuous young girl and caused more than a couple of small accidents along our street as we hung out on summer days in front of my house, visible to the boys driving by.

Across the side street lived Mr. Clark, the alleged pedophile. Nobody knew what to make of him. From my front porch, I would watch as young girls walked by and he'd call out, "How you doin', sugah?" Sometimes I'd be standing out front with Kim when Mr. Clark would come home. He would drive up in his Sanford and Son truck, hop out, and yell over to us, "How you doin' baby? Come here. Let me give you a dollar." Kim would never go, but I wanted that dollar. I'd run over to Mr. Clark and reach for the dollar bill while he'd try to put a lip-lock on me. But I was always too quick, turning my head so all he got was my cheek. To my knowledge, that's as far as Mr. Clark went with anybody, but I remember Mother saying, "Something ain't right with that man. You stop taking money from him."

Anyway, we did our best to avoid Mr. Clark whenever we could. Otherwise, the neighborhood was safe enough. It was a decent, working-class neighborhood and if we lacked for wealth, I never noticed. We lived comfortably enough on Mama's wages from the Kroger, and Mother's social security. The house was a conventional, red-brick home built in 1921. Four bedrooms and a single bathroom. Lots of homes were built in our neighborhood in the early part of the twentieth century. Shawnee neighborhood in western Louisville sprang up with the completion of Shawnee Park in 1892, a 284-acre park a mile west of our house that rests on the banks of the Ohio River. Kim and I would often walk or ride our bikes to the park. Sometimes I'd go with Lisa. Less than two blocks to the east of the house runs Interstate 264, which represents the eastern border of the neighborhood.

Shawnee was mostly white until the 1960s. Little by little it became integrated. Then, in May of 1968, a few weeks after the assassination of Martin

Luther King, Jr., riots broke out in the nearby Parkland neighborhood. A crowd had gathered to protest the reinstatement of a white cop who'd been suspended for beating a black man. With the MLK assassination still fresh on everyone's mind, the protest turned violent and the mayor ended up calling in the National Guard. After that, many long-time white residents left Western Louisville, leaving it mostly Black today, and it was right around this time that Mother and Mama bought the house. I remember a nice, older white couple living in the Clark's house before they came along and another white gentleman, appropriately named Mr. White, living next door to them, the last holdouts.

I had friends to play with and stayed out of trouble as a young girl, and I'm sure by all outward appearances, I probably seemed like a typical, well-adjusted child. But when I consider those days, it strikes me clearly that I was not especially happy. There is nothing in particular that stands out as to why this was, aside from Mama giving me the blues all the time. Reports from my teachers indicate that I was a sweet kid and eager to learn. But my fifth grade teacher, Miss Bishop, wrote of her concern that I was "feeling bad." My sixth grade teacher, Miss McShan, might have helped illuminate the problem a year later with her report card comment that I was "lacking confidence."

This doesn't seem surprising. Thankfully, I had Miss Barbara, Miss Clark, and Miss Bailey to give me a little of that, because it sure didn't come from Mama. I loved Mama and I'm sure she loved me. We were mother/daughter so we were obliged to love each other. Was there anything more between us than obligation? As the years go on, it gets harder and harder to say.

Chapter 4

The Outside World

Classroom work was hard for me. I could never focus. I wanted to learn, but I struggled. Considering my future Navy responsibilities, it seems impossible that I almost flunked home economics but whenever we were assigned to prepare something, I couldn't keep my mind fixed on the recipe card instructions. I had similar problems with other subjects and it made me frustrated, even angry. I was always late for class because I dreaded having to sit there like a dummy while my friends and classmates all did well. And so I got in trouble for being late and I got in trouble for doing poorly, all of which made me even more frustrated. Couldn't the teachers understand? Didn't they see that I wanted to do well but just couldn't? For a while, I became class clown, making the other kids laugh as a way to camouflage what I thought was my lack of smarts.

Sometimes the trouble followed me home. Mama kept her pulse on the goings-on at school from the people coming through her check-out lane at the Kroger. And if they didn't spill the beans about some kind of trouble I got in, I could always count on my brother Ricky to snitch. Kim would always say, "I wish he'd get a life and stop selling us out."

My salvation at school, the one thing that kept me coming back, was non-classroom related. I was on the basketball team and basketball, unlike classwork, was something I was good at. At least *I* thought I was good. I liked sports. I'd always been something of a tomboy, a little rough around the edges and not afraid to mix it up a little. One time, a neighbor kid named Wayne Sullivan came walking past our house and said, "Hey, Sharon Rucker, I just seen your bike over at Jerry Reed's house." Now, Jerry Reed was kind of a goofy kid and I'd always given him a hard time. But this was way out of line. *Really? You're going to steal my fifteen-inch, Florida-orange AMF Scorcher?* Jerry Reed done stole the wrong bike.

I marched over to his house, went around back, and saw my bike through the gate in his backyard. I knocked on the front door. "You steal my bike?" I said when he answered. Before he could reply, I punched him hard in the chest and then went and grabbed my bike and rode home. He never touched my bike again.

And so sports came kind of instinctively to me. Not that I didn't have to work at basketball. At first, just like in class, I'd find myself having trouble paying attention. More than once I got popped upside the head with the ball from a pass that I simply hadn't noticed was coming my way. Here I was, a power forward who would forget where to post. Miss Anglin, our coach, worked with me, though, and taught me, among other things, how to use my body—my butt in particular—to back up and block out a defending player. Once I got better, I had less trouble staying focused. The game seemed to come more naturally and I didn't have to think about it as much. And I liked the camaraderie of the team. My last name was Rucker and my teammates called me "Ruck," and it was nice to hear "What up Ruck?" when I'd show up for practice. I felt accepted. I felt as if I belonged.

Of course I had friends off the court, but none closer than Kim. We'd go to neighborhood parties and get-togethers down at the park and meet up with other kids. We often had sleepovers at her house, never having them at mine. Kim respected Mama but she knew that the woman everyone thought was so sweet wasn't always so sweet to me. Mama had a boyfriend one time named Mr. Otha who had four mostly grown sons. Sometimes, she'd drop Kim and me off at his house and the two would go out somewhere. We'd hang out with the sons, listening to old-school jams and shooting pool in the basement. It seemed fine at the time, but although Tony, Bubba, Butch, and Gary were like brothers to me, I now look back and wonder how Mama could have just left Kim and me alone with four young men. Normally, she wouldn't trust me to be alone with a single boy, let alone four of them.

Nothing happened with those guys, but I did have a few boyfriends in those days. Bob White was my first love. He was a couple of years older than me and fun to hang with. We were close, but too young to be serious. We'd kiss out by the back steps while Mama would call down, "Sharon, where you at?!" Just out by the back door, I'd say. Later, there was Harry Pitts, our high school star quarterback. He broke his leg during a game one time and I can still remember him coming over to my place in a cast above his knee, driving his Ford Pinto. Now *that* was love.

In my senior year, I went to the prom with Joe Parker, a star on the boys basketball team, but we went as friends. Greg Page, a boxer who would go on to become WBA Heavyweight Champion in the mid-eighties, had graduated from Central the year before. He still hung around the school on game nights, like a lot of previous graduates would, all of them giving the current crop of athletes a hard time. One night he told me that I should go to the prom with Joe. "You both have too many to choose from," he said.

"Just go together." Joe and I thought it was a good idea. Miss Barbara made my prom dress, which Mama never said a word about.

I had boyfriends but the only sex I had was the one-day stand with that got-me-in-jail, wish-I'd-never-met-his-ass Rasheeno. Otherwise, I was abstinent. I might have gotten into some trouble at school for being late to class or for failing a test or something, but I never went looking for *real* trouble. Outside of maybe smoking a cigarette or two out behind the portable classroom buildings, I was a good girl with enough sense not to do anything too stupid. Girls around me, including Kim, were getting pregnant, but not me. Kim was fifteen at the time and she asked that I be with her when she broke the news to Miss Barbara. (Of course I was, although it turned out that Miss Barbara already knew by the time I got there; mothers know these things.) It's not that I didn't fool around, but I was smart enough to ask Mama if I could get on the pill, just in case I ever decided to try it again. Fortunately, she had no problem with the idea, knowing that, even despite being a tomboy, I was developing into a curvy piece of eye-candy just like her. And from her own experience at Central High, I'm sure she believed that abstinence wasn't realistic.

In my high school years, I saw more of Daddy. Most times, I could find him at Vermont Liquors over on 34th and Vermont. If he wasn't there, his buddies would always tell me where I could find him. Going into Vermont Liquors to see Daddy was nothing to me. I'd stick my head in the door, the entire place reeking of stale alcohol and cigarette smoke, and the old men would yell, "Yo, Hawk, Sharon's out here!" Daddy was always glad to see me. He lived with my older brother for a time on 38th and Market, not far from Shawnee Park and I'd see him there, too.

Daddy made it to a couple of my basketball games. Mama never did. Other engagements took priority. Frequently, she'd be off at a golf or bowling tournament with Mr. Otha. She worked, of course, but Mama liked to entertain and loved attention. Marelilly was popular and if she didn't go out somewhere, often enough she'd have people over. On weekends mostly, there would be folks in the kitchen late in the evenings drinking Old Forester whiskey, smoking Viceroy cigarettes, and eating Limburger cheese. The next day, that Old Forester would be back in the dining room cabinet where my cousin Cynthia and I would often sneak a taste when we knew Mama would be out for the evening.

High school graduation got closer and my future awaited, but I didn't have any serious plans. I imagined working in a bank or something. A steady job. Nothing glamorous. I'd stay in Louisville obviously, because Louisville was all I knew. But way in the back of my mind, I had the idea of seeing other places. As it happened, when I was a little younger, I'd taken a trip to see my Aunt Ann. Ann had been married to Daddy's brother Robert. Uncle Robert served in the army and was stationed at Fort Monmouth, New Jersey where he met my auntie. They married, had my cousins Cookie and Flip, and eventually moved to Louisville. I was ten when Uncle Robert died and Aunt Ann moved back to New Jersey with my cousins. I kept in touch with them. Aunt Ann told me I was always welcome to come see them and when I was fourteen, I asked Mama if I could go. I saved my allowance and with a little help from Mama and Aunt Ann, I bought a plane ticket and off I went, all alone on an Eastern Airlines flight, my first time on an airplane, my first time out of Louisville. It was exciting and the adrenaline I felt on my first flight helped me overcome any jitters I might have had about flying. The adrenaline kept me focused.

Aunt Ann lived in Tinton Falls, about an hour south of Manhattan. Tinton Falls was also close to Monmouth Beach. It was there where I first gazed out at the ocean. I'd only ever seen pictures and I couldn't stop staring at the waves and found myself mesmerized by the vastness of the water, extending all the way to the horizon, and disappearing against the blue-gray sky.

My aunt spoiled me, making my favorite dinner—spaghetti and meat balls—and whatever else I asked for. Cookie, about nine years older than me, took me to Atlantic City and we strolled along the famous boardwalk where I had my first foot-long hot dog and shaved ice. New Jersey, it seemed to me, had everything that Louisville didn't.

It had something else, too, that at that time I hadn't been exposed to: people from different walks of life and different ethnicities. Cookie had a party for me while I was there and invited some friends and neighbors over, some of whom were of Puerto Rican descent and others of Jamaican descent. I'd never spent any time with people of other ethnicities and Cookie's friends introduced me to other parts of the world.

For the duration of the trip, I felt I was out of my element. But being out of my element was a wonderful place to be.

This is where my interest in traveling was born.

And so after trying college at the University of Louisville and dropping out, and after the Kroger incident, it struck me that getting out of the 'Ville and seeing something of the outside world might be a way for me to carve out a better future than working in a store or a bank or somewhere close to home. At this point I was a college dropout and a reformed thief. And so the next thing I knew, I was on that flight—the second one of my young life—to Orlando, Florida to the Naval Training Center. The flight to New Jersey showed me there was an outside world. The flight to

Orlando would put me on a path that would show me that world.

CHAPTER 5

BOOT CAMP

Besides those neighborhood parties and hanging down at Shawnee Park, there were the parties that I held in my own basement and there was no denying that these were the best. My childhood friend, William Turner, AKA "Big Man the DJ," always had those parties jammin' with Rick James's "Bustin' Out," and Parliament Funkadelic's "Dog Catcher." It was standing room only, with the music blaring and everybody having a great time. It was just such a party that Mama let me have as a going-away party on the Saturday night before I left for the Navy. Everyone was saying, "Sharon Rucker, I can't believe you going!" But by then, I was so excited about my future prospects that I couldn't imagine *not* going.

Four days later, April Fool's Day, I flew to Recruit Training Command in Orlando for eight weeks of Navy boot camp, where the excitement wore off some. Not because of the rigors of boot camp, but because of the feelings of guilt I'd carried with me from Louisville. I'd left Mama all alone, or at least that's what it felt like. Of course she still had Mother, although she was aging, and she still had my brothers and she still had all of her friends and those kitchen get-togethers with the Old Forester and the smelly Limburger cheese, not to mention her boyfriend and the bowling and golf tournaments.

But Mama had a way of making me feel like I was always doing something wrong or, at the least, not measuring up to some level of expectation that she had. When I'd come home from the recruitment office to tell Mama I was joining the Navy, she said, "What do you want to do that for?" I even had Petty Officer First Class Tyrone Wilson come by to talk with her, telling her of the opportunities the Navy would offer me. Eventually, she admitted, "Maybe it'll be good for you." I could have read her response as favorable, but for some reason, I didn't. Looking back, I think I was still reeling from the Kroger incident, still looking for forgiveness, still wanting to please Mama. Then again, looking back, it seems as though Mama understood this on some level. Maybe it was too much of a temptation for her not to take advantage of the dynamic. No, she wasn't critical of my decision to join the Navy, but, then again, neither was she very encouraging about it. Once again, I was left without her approval.

Miss Barbara seemed to understand the situation. Before I'd left, I talked to her about leaving Mama. "Miss Barbara, I don't know if I should go," I told her. "I'm really worried about leaving. Who's going to keep the house together while I'm away and she's working?"

"Your Mama is gonna be just fine," Miss Barbara assured me.

Ms. Clark said more or less the same thing. "Baby, you go on and live your life," she told me.

Mama did have one sincere thing to say to me before I left, and she'd repeat it many times in the years that followed: "Watch as well as pray, Sharon." And I would do so. I'd watch. And I'd pray. Prayer was important to me. Mother used to remind us of 1 Thessalonians 5:16: "Pray without ceasing." I took this to heart, through boot camp and beyond. My prayers were simple—Lord, please help me through this; Lord, don't let me screw this up—but they were near constant. On Sundays at the Recruit Training Command, religious services were available and you could have your pick—Catholic, Protestant, or whatever. Sunday was my favorite day of the week at boot camp.

The rest of the days were marked by a lot of regimentation and hard work, pretty much as you'd expect. Reveille was every morning at zero-five-hundred, followed by breakfast and then out to the grinder, a huge lot where we would march in formation and do drill commands with our weapons. After a couple of hours of that, it was lunch and then a variety of afternoon activities including having rack (bunk) inspections, locker inspections, shoeshine inspections, pistol inspections, uniform inspections, and every other kind of inspection. We did fire drills. One day we did a gas chamber drill where we had to make use of gas masks. Of course, we attended classes on basic seamanship. One week was "work week" where each recruit was assigned to a specific work detail, maybe galley detail or trash pickup. We'd have "field days" where we had to clean the barracks from top to bottom. (Like a lot of longtime sailors, I still refer to the act of cleaning my residence as "field dayin'.") The days were long, but they all ended the same way—with *Taps* playing and everyone hitting the rack.

The petty officers in charge (POICs)—the equivalents of drill sergeants in the Army or Marines—were PO Fleming and PO Pratt. Everyone liked PO Pratt. She was cool people. PO Fleming? Not so much. Petty Officer Fleming was hardcore. She expected a lot, was not one to be played with, and did not suffer fools. We loved to hate her, but we had no choice but to follow her orders smartly and, down the road, I found myself impressed with how strong-minded she was. How could I have known then that instead of becoming PO Pratt, I'd go on to become PO Fleming?

Overall, I liked boot camp. I endured it just fine. Besides church every Sunday, the thing that helped me the most was that because of my work experience, going back to the Walgreens, I was already used to being bitched at, so I knew boot camp would be a piece of cake. I was enthusiastic about the Navy from the start and felt as though I belonged. I guess it's not surprising that I was made section leader. There were ten recruits to a section and there were six sections in ranks. Having section leaders made it easier for the petty officers in charge to do their jobs. As a section leader, my role was to make sure my people were squared away for uniform inspections, check to see that they had made their racks correctly, muster them for chow, and drill them on their general orders and Navy core values, like honor, courage, and commitment, along with the proper procedures of everything from how to salute the flag to how to request permission to board a ship.

The other thing I liked about boot camp was that it didn't give me much time to think about home and Mama. Even though Miss Barbara had assured me everything would be okay, I was still feeling guilty about leaving. And Mama didn't help any. When I'd call home, she'd remind me that the collect calls were costing her money.

And so boot camp was a nice escape, even the time when they shoved us all into the water, and from a very high platform. We had to prove that we could float, obviously a necessary skill in a military branch that more or less lives on the ocean. They pushed us into fourteen feet of water and we had to stay afloat for several minutes. Interestingly, you never had to prove that you could swim, just float long enough to be rescued. This was a good thing for me, because I couldn't swim. In fact, I would go on to serve the next twenty years in the US Navy without knowing how to swim. If swimming had been a requirement, I'm sure I would have found a way to do it. I wanted in that bad. But as it was, I'd serve on ships that sailed both the Pacific Ocean and the Mediterranean Sea and I'd look out over those vast waters and think to myself, if we go down, it's all over for me. The funny thing is, one of the things I'd bark out to my duty sections if we weren't running a general quarters (GQ) drill properly was, "If we ever go down, I don't want none of y'all on *my* damn team!" Meanwhile, what they didn't know was that with my inability to swim, they wouldn't have wanted me on their team, either. But I did pass that float test. The fact that I couldn't swim was something I kept a secret until, well, until just now.

Boot camp was eight weeks and, all in all, it gave me something I would eventually realize I needed in life more than anything else: something to focus on. It gave me direction. It gave me specific tasks that I could concentrate my energies upon. All my life, I had needed that kind of direction, though I didn't know why. Other people—normal people—could focus on several things at once and seemingly with little effort. But for me, staying on task was difficult. The Navy made it easier. I welcomed the discipline and I flourished like I never had before.

Chapter 6

Mess Management Specialist

When it came to what field I wanted to be in, or rating, as the Navy calls it, my initial thinking was that I wanted accounting or maybe supply, figuring I could be an SK (storekeeper), managing inventory. This was Mama's influence, my observation of her in her Kroger checkout lane ringing up customers with precise efficiency. It might also have partly been because I liked putting things in order and keeping everything organized. I needed things to be like that. I needed order. The structure, after all, was a big part of what I liked about the Navy.

But the Navy had other ideas about my rating. My Armed Services Vocational Aptitude Battery, or ASVAB (the armed services love initials and acronyms), which was the test I took when I was recruited, revealed I was qualified in four ratings—radioman (RM), ship's serviceman (SH), yeoman (YN), and mess management specialist (MS). All of these required attention to detail, which is interesting to me now when I think about it.

The last one especially appealed to me. It meant working in the galley as a cook and I had always liked to bake, even though I'd had trouble with those recipe cards in home economics. In fact, the neighborhood girls on my block sometimes called me Betty Crocker. I'd sometimes bake cookies for a few of the fellas from our high school basketball team and we'd all hang out on my porch. I guess the nickname was a form of bullying, but I didn't mind it. After all, the boys were on my porch, not theirs. And so I chose MS and after boot camp, the Navy sent me to San Diego for Accession Training, or "A" school, to learn my new job.

A School had a lot of the same elements as boot camp, but most of my work consisted of learning food preparation and sanitation, as well as learning all about food service equipment. We learned the cookware—size and depth and volume of all the pots and pans. We learned the Naval Supply Systems Command (NAVSUP) Form 1090, which was the daily food preparation worksheet. We learned about preparing menus for a five-week cycle that included breakfast, lunch, dinner, plus midnight rations for the guys standing late watches. Most importantly, we had to learn recipe cards and portion control, all based on one-hundred portions. So if you were serving 50 or 500 or 5,000, you needed to do the math to determine how much of the ingredients to use so that you could requisition what you needed from the JOD—the "Jack of the Dust," the nickname for the MS in charge of food supplies.

I could see that as an MS, I was going to be in for a lot of work. I welcomed it.

Two weeks after reporting to A School, I got some bad news from home. Before I had left Louisville, I had a sense that Mother wasn't doing well. She'd moved out of our home by then and had been living with her son Henry. She needed the extra attention. We noticed little things while she was living with us, like her putting the milk in the kitchen cabinet or the sugar in the refrigerator. Whether she got the extra attention she needed at her son's house, I can't say. I didn't spend a lot of time visiting her there and so I'm sure I didn't see the worst of the dementia. After I'd left for the Navy, Mother had a stroke and ended up in Summerfield nursing home. She died in June of 1981 following another stroke. It set me back a week in A School, but I was allowed to go home for the funeral, which I attended in uniform. But I was mad at Mother. Her death had come too quickly and she had left without giving me a chance to tell her how much I loved her or to thank her for being my Godfearing rock.

Back in San Diego, I finished A School and reported to my first duty station—Naval Air Station Point Mugu in California, between Ventura and Santa Monica. Point Mugu was the airfield that Reagan used during his presidency on his visits to his Santa Barbara ranch. I was assigned to the enlisted dining facility, or the EDF as we called it, as a galley cook, responsible for the daily food preparation, for maintaining the food service equipment, and for all galley spaces and storerooms, keeping everything clean and sanitary. I also worked as an EDF cashier.

Somewhere along the way, I acquired the nickname "Shay." I liked it. With a new name, I felt a little like a new person. I've been Shay ever since.

At the EDF, Petty Officer First Class George Bullecer was my LPO—Leading Petty Officer. My boss. George was in charge of the mess—the cashiers, the cooks, everybody. He was mess deck master at arms, and a squared-away guy. He was the first LPO I had that didn't treat me like a subordinate. Always teaching and looking out for us, George taught me that you could be both a supervisor and a friend to your troops.

As an MS, my responsibilities also included barracks management. And so at one point, I was rotated to the barracks, or BEQ (Bachelor's Enlisted Quarters), where my LPO was MR1 Jefferson, a machinist repairman who'd been assigned as leading petty officer for the BEQ. We called him JJ and JJ was easy-going and lenient. His motto was, "Let's get the work done, ya'll, so we can go home." At lunch, he let us go to the Acey-Deucey club where we'd knock back some cold ones. I had good shipmates on the base and these were good times. Once, I even participated in the first annual culinary competition for all the mess specialists in the various commands around Ventura County. I didn't win anything, but it was still a fun experience.

I spent two years at Point Mugu. Mama hadn't missed a beat in reminding me about the collect calls as if they were a terrible inconvenience to her. By then, I was sending money home to cover the calls, but Mama couldn't seem to resist needling me with a little guilt anytime she got the chance. One time I called home when our insurance man happened to be at the house. Mama put him on. I expected he wanted to know how the Navy was treating me and if I was doing okay, but instead he said, "Sharon, why are you sending money home to your boyfriend instead of your mama? You shouldn't be sending money home to boys! Your mama needs your help here."

Why would she have told him that? I wondered to myself. My paygrade was E-3: Seaman. "I don't have any money to send to no boyfriend," I told him, as if I had to defend myself to the insurance man.

She spoke other untruths to others back home, or at least purposely misled them. Often, she'd ask someone, "Have you heard from Sharon?" as if she hadn't heard from me herself, even if we had chatted that morning on the phone. Sometimes she'd just flat out lie to aunts and uncles and tell them I wasn't keeping in touch with her at all.

Mama caused me such anxiety and depression. She'd caused me anxiety and depression as a young girl living in her house, and now she was causing me anxiety and depression as an adult in the Navy. I covered it up with my work. I probably needed to talk to someone, but in the service you didn't want to appear weak. There was a stigma back in those days and I didn't want to take the chance of broadcasting my emotional problems to the Navy. But I did have a homeboy from Louisville who lived in Ventura. Kenneth Pearson's mother and my mother were friends, and it gave me someone to talk to about Mama. Kenneth understood, but then he'd say, "Well, that's your mama, baby. We only get one mama." And so I'd try to be patient and understanding with Mama which in hindsight probably just caused me more anxiety.

I ended my time at Point Mugu as a Petty Officer Third Class. My evaluation that led to making rank reported, among other things, that my "positive attitude, sound judgment, and leadership" motivated my peers and subordinates "to continually achieve a high level of customer satisfaction." But there was also a notation that I occasionally needed "to be more flexible and determined in tackling disagreeable tasks," a diplomatic way of saying, "We need to monitor this hothead." The truth is, I'd sometimes feel frustrated by not being understood and that frustration showed itself.

In fact, at Point Mugu, while working in the barracks, I told off a lieutenant one time who had taken issue with some of us using a phone that was on his desk. It was a DSN line meaning that long-distance calls were free. "What's the big deal?!" I shouted at him, losing my temper. "You let others use the phone, but my duty section can't?!" Of course, a third-class petty officer is never supposed to speak to a lieutenant that way. I had a few other choice words for him, too, and he lowered my mark in personal behavior on my next eval. This hurt me for my advancement to the next paygrade. It was the only occasion when I didn't make rank my first time up.

And he wasn't the only one I had an issue with. In the galley, they often called me "recipe card cook," forever giving me a hard time because of my obsessiveness with the recipe cards. But being obsessive was the only way I could focus and pay attention to detail. They couldn't understand that, which, in fairness, I didn't really understand at the time either. Later, I would learn the term "hyperfocus"—the idea of overly concentrating on something to the exclusion of all else, a common ADHD symptom.

It didn't help that I tended toward perfectionism anyway. This had been ingrained in me by Mama's constant disappointment and disapproval. I had to do things perfectly, and I found myself demanding perfection from my troops, especially if I thought they were gundecking, Navy slang for doing something half-assed.

One time, I almost lost it to the point of wanting to punch one of the guys. But I knew fighting wasn't going to help me advance, so I did what I often did when I felt myself losing my temper. I went out on the back deck and cried. Then I shook that shit off and headed back to the galley. But I maintained my obsessiveness. Nobody in my entire career ever had to remind me to pay attention to detail.

Somewhere along the line, I toughened up. And I decided that the best revenge was to go full steam ahead, making rank, while the ones who'd made fun of me were still trying to make rank and not being very successful at it. For all I know, they're still trying.

Point Mugu was shore duty, but the Navy required sea/shore rotation for all Navy sailors. Eventually, I had to report for sea duty. But there was just one problem. Women weren't allowed on ships back in those days, and wouldn't be until the early '90s. It was a screwed up policy and I thought so at the time. I was ready to be a sea sailor. But when you're in the military, you go with the flow, and, as we'd always say, "carry on smartly." For women back in the 1980s, sea duty could be achieved through service on a base outside of the United States. The Navy considered this to be equivalent.

I had several places to choose from and settled on Puerto Rico. I remembered meeting Cookie's Puerto Rican friends at the party she had thrown for me in Jersey. In November of 1983, I reported to Naval Station Roosevelt Roads, Puerto Rico. Today, the site is the home of a public airport, but before the base closed in 2004, it had been a Naval base since Franklin Roosevelt ordered its creation in 1940.

Not long after I arrived, I took leave to fly home. Daddy, who was living with my brother, had fallen down the basement stairs and had suffered serious head trauma. He was conscious, but didn't recognize anybody. I knew that sometimes Daddy would play possum, too, keeping his eyes closed if he didn't want to see someone. But when I got to the hospital and walked into his room, I gave Daddy a kiss on his forehead and he opened his eyes and recognized me. I was able to return to Puerto Rico, so happy that Daddy still knew me, and satisfied that he was going to be okay.

At Roosevelt Roads I started out with basically the same duties as what I'd had at Point Mugu. But I had trouble getting along with some of the other cooks in the galley. I couldn't seem to control the growing frustrations within, which led to angry outbursts. In turn, this led to others thinking that I felt I was somehow better than everybody else, a perception that would dog me throughout my career. What they didn't know was that I often felt the opposite. I worked constantly to try to measure up to standards that I was certain I fell short of. But outwardly, it resulted in me often acting like an angry tyrant, always raising hell about this or that.

Later in life, I would come to understand what was behind those feelings of mine. At the time, with no awareness or understanding of my ADHD issues, my solution was to ask for a transfer and I ended up in the MWR Department. The Morale, Welfare, and Recreation program was a quality-of-life program to support the service members with leisure activities. It included all of the sailors' recreational facilities—arcade games, a bowling alley, candy and soda machines, and the like. There were boat and kayak rentals in the marina, too. I worked for the command comptroller, internal control division, performing such tasks as disbursing cash, verifying daily receipts, making bank deposits, and preparing daily activity reports. The MWR spots were contracted out, managed by a civilian, a gentleman by the name of Harvey Conrad and so I essentially worked for him.

Harvey was from Florida and he and his wife Betty were a laid-back couple and loads of fun to be with. Harvey would pick me up and we'd go around to the various recreation offices and vending machines, collecting the week's revenue. Then he'd take me back to my office where I'd tally up all the money, running it through the dollar and coin machines. On weekends, Harvey and Betty would often invite me to their home in San Juan.

All of my coworkers were civilians, mostly Puerto Rican, and I learned to appreciate Puerto Rican cuisine and café con leche. I loved interacting with different people. But I made friends on the base, too. We'd hang out on the base's private beaches, and our married shipmates who lived in base housing would often host get-togethers for us singles who lived in the barracks.

But my temper was still ever-present, always just below the surface. One night outside of a club, some guy said the wrong thing to me. Today, I couldn't even tell you what it was but it was apparently enough because I punched him, spraining my thumb in the process, but making the punch count. By the time he tried to swing back, Shore Patrol had stepped in and broken up the fight.

Overall, however, my service at Roosey Roads, as we called it (pronounced "Rosy"), was outstanding, at least that's what it said on my evals. I was "conscientious," "highly motivated," and "cheerful while working." In fact, I was "Sailor of the Month" for a couple of months and nominated a couple of other times. Sailor of the Month was a big deal to a peon sailor in the Navy. My final eval was a perfect 4.0 and I was given the "strongest recommendation for retention and advancement."

That was cool with me. I knew almost from the start of my service in the Navy that I was going to stay in for a while. While in Puerto Rico, I decided to make it official. I reenlisted right on the beach. I had taken the Navy-wide exam for advancement and passed and I proudly stitched the Petty Officer Second Class Mess Management Specialist badge onto my left sleeve. When I reenlisted, I had a choice. I could reenlist for two years, four years, or six years. I chose six. I'd been in four, so that would put me at ten years and make me a "lifer." The Navy was now my life.

CHAPTER 7

JAY

In August, 1985, after making Petty Officer Second Class, I reported for duty at Naval Amphibious Base (NAB) Coronado in San Diego. While there, I did more than just naval duty. All along, I had wanted to further my education and I enrolled in any classes the Navy had to offer. At NAB, I attended "C" school—advanced training in my field, including food production and food service records. But I took night classes off base too. I came to realize that if I accumulated my schooling—took my high school transcripts, the work I'd done at the University of Louisville, the military classes, plus the night schooling—I could roll it all into an associate degree, or even higher.

When I put it all together, I was surprised by the amount of schooling I had done. My senior chief, Rick Mendoza, called me a "career student," and I guess I was. I enrolled in the Regents External Degree

Program of the University of the State of New York (now called Excelsior College)—a distance-learning program under Navy contract—and I earned my associate degree in Science and Liberal Arts. Eventually, I would go on to earn my Bachelors. All of it would help. One of my LPOs would say, "If you study long, you put it on." I would take that advice and run with it for the remainder of my Navy career.

Something else happened at NAB too. I met a guy. Jay was a boatswain's mate who came to the enlisted dining facility. He'd walk up to the cashier's window and he'd always have something smart and cocky to say. I was a higher pay grade than Jay and he'd joke about how I thought I was running the show at the EDF. I'd joke right back and say, "Watch your mouth, shipmate. You want to eat today?"

Jay asked me out and before long we were seeing each other regularly. We'd go to Balboa Park, a public park in San Diego with green areas and walking paths, restaurants, museums, and the famous San Diego Zoo. We'd go to Coronado Beach, too, and Seaport Village, a cool waterfront shopping complex with eclectic shops and cafes. We'd roller skate in Spanish Landing Park near the San Diego airport and watch the planes take off and land.

We fell in love. We dated about a year before we got married at the San Diego Courthouse in September of 1987. Jay bought Mama a plane ticket and she came to our little wedding. I wrote to Daddy about Jay and he wrote back saying, "He better watch himself!"

Jay and I moved off base, renting a nice apartment in Chula Vista. It was my very first apartment and I loved being married and grown up. I felt as if I were now out from Mama's shadow. Somehow, with Jay, I felt safe from her, or at least freed up from the constant mental drama. He even intercepted some of her phone calls, making it difficult for her to impose her guilt trips upon me. It had gotten to the point where talking to her had become a frickin' chore. She would talk about friends of hers, like her friend Emma, just to tell me about all the wonderful things Emma's children would do for Emma. I dreaded those phone calls. Jay started answering them, telling Mama that I was out of the house or asleep.

Jay was a great guy. I was crazy about him. He was good with money too. And he worked hard. Often he'd take a watch for one of the other sailors. There was always somebody looking for a little downtime who'd be willing to pay someone to take their duty. Jay was always taking duties. He helped me get out of the debt that I'd gotten myself into, a result of my poor spending habits—my impulsivity wasn't getting any better with age.

Neither was my hyperactivity. I'd be going in ten different directions at once. I'd start a project, maybe start cleaning the kitchen, when suddenly it would occur to me that the dining room needed to be cleaned first. I'd drop the kitchen cleaning, then focus on the dining room, until it would occur to me that the laundry needed to be done and the next thing I knew, I'd be throwing clothes in the washing machine. I'd go from room to room, starting and stopping activities and sometimes forgetting what I'd just been working on. And then in the midst of it all, I would realize that I needed to pick up some things at the grocery store. Off I went. I must have looked like the Tasmanian Devil whirling around the apartment.

Jay would make me stop and slow down. "You just stay right there on that couch," he'd say. "You don't need to go nowhere. You need something, you just ask me." Twenty-six years old and I needed someone to put me in timeout. But Jay was good for me like that. Often times, I'd bring my anger issues home from work. I'd come home fighting mad and take my frustration out on Jay, but he remained laid-back and drama-free. (Thanks, Jay.)

My service time at NAB was productive, though strangely I don't remember just how productive it really was. It always seemed to me that I couldn't stay focused, but somehow, before I left, I was nominated as South Bay Council Navy League "Enlisted Woman of the Year." The Navy League was a nonprofit civilian group founded in 1902 under President Theodore

Roosevelt and was an advocacy group that supported America's sea services.

From NAB Coronado, I reported for duty in
June of 1988 to Naval Air Station, Agana, Guam.
There, I served as LPO of the Bachelor Enlisted
Quarters. I moved up a paygrade, too, earning "Superiors" across the board in my advancement exam,
a rare achievement for advancement exams. In fact,
another sailor would later do the same thing and
end up in the *Navy Times*. There was no such fanfare for me. The sailor happened to be white and a
dude. (Just sayin'.)

The upswing was reporting to Guam as a First
Class Petty Officer. Jay came to Guam, too. We had
submitted a NAVPERS 1306/7, a standard Navy
form for submissions of requests to higher author-
ities. We had requested spouse co-location. Whenever possible, the Navy does its best to keep spouses
together and our request had been granted. Jay's
orders were to report to the *USS Niagara Falls*,
homeported in Guam. We left our car, Jay's 1987
Maxima, back in the States, with Jay thinking that
the salt air would be bad for it in Guam. We had a
two-car garage built in Mama's backyard and began
sending money home each month to pay for it.
That car would become the Sunday go-to-church
car for Mama and Miss Emma, though Mama never
uttered a word of appreciation for it.

At the BEQ, I had to deal with a prick of a supply officer. Lieutenant Peace was a short little redneck who was always giving me and my people a hard time. "Peace" was a hell of a name for a hell-raiser. I ran a request to see our commanding officer, Captain O'Connor, about Peace's sorry leadership. Like all requests, it had to go through the chain of command. This meant Lieutenant Peace got the request first, providing him a chance to give me a jab when he had to sign off on it. "The captain's gonna slam-dunk you and so am I," he said. I mentioned this to Captain O'Connor who smiled and said, "Well, consider yourself slam-dunked, MS1. Now, tell me what's going on in your division." It was good to get it all off my chest. The captain spoke with Peace and Peace did throttle back a bit. But I still had to look out for my people and keep a watchful eye on Peace, all the while remaining respectful. It became tiring and I started getting migraines in the mornings on my way to the base. Eventually, I requested a transfer from the barracks to the galley and that's where I would serve out my stay at NAS.

In the galley, they didn't really need another first-class petty officer because they already had MS1 Pamela Gosnell as LPO. But we made it work. I liked Pam. She was from Arkansas, which was obvious from her accent. And she was smart. She knew the Navy publication NAVSUP P-486, basically the foodservice bible, frontward and backward, rattling off parts of it like she was spitting out her social security number. She thought highly of me, too, which surprised me because she was so smart. But we were both team builders and neither one of us cared about one-upping the other. I was finding this to be rare. It seemed everyone was constantly trying to compete at everything. In fact, Pam was always trying to calm me down whenever I'd get upset about someone or something. She'd be a mellow counterweight to my anger. "Now, Sharon," she'd say with her slow Southern drawl, "don't get yourself all riled up about it."

Overall, I flourished in Guam and did well with my responsibilities. At one point, I was the central assignment records and desk supervisor of the BEQ, assigning quarters to permanent personnel, but also to the many transient enlisted personnel and officers who would come through Guam for training or on their way elsewhere. Sometimes this meant having to be quick on your feet. Once, with less than twelve hours' notice, I needed to berth 150 sailors for a training exercise. But I thrived on making things happen. I liked keeping busy. I put in extra hours on and off duty. And I found other ways to keep myself occupied, like joining the chapel choir or holding off-duty study sessions with my juniors.

In the choir, we would sing at the base chapel and for command events. Sometimes we'd have combined church services with Andersen Air Force Base. I enjoyed these services. We'd be praising God together—what a joy—but in the spirit of friendly rivalry, I loved watching the Air Force soloists try to one-up the Navy soloists, me being one of them. One of my shipmates, Joyce Nyhaug, is making gospel hits to this day. That girl can sing.

I'd join or start a choir at almost every command that I was assigned to throughout my entire career, including an international gospel choir at Jebel Ali, United Arab Emirates. I served on the *USS McKee* and we joined forces with the *USS Vancouver*, an amphibious transport ship, or "dock" as it was called. I directed. The Marines from the *Vancouver* merged vocals with us and it was fun having those grunts under my direction.

On Guam, a few of us sailors from various commands and squadrons formed a Black history month committee. The EDF served a traditional African-American meal, as we did for every ethnic-celebrated month. We held a talent/modeling show too. I modeled, and sang Natalie Cole's "Inseparable." I sang it for Jay, my love bug who was out to sea at the time.

I also volunteered to help out with picnics for Navy SEALs. One time, I was given the responsibility of assisting with a special breakfast for the president of the Philippines. I kept fit, too, and received a commendation for achieving an "Outstanding" grade twice in a row on the Navy's Physical Readiness Test. In all my evals, I scored perfect 4.0s, which, looking back, I can see elevated my spirits. It was gratifying to see comments like "energetic and motivated" and "tireless devotion to duty." During my time in Guam, I had a hard-working crew and we racked up several letters of appreciation from the CO as well as the commandant.

Again, however, as at NAB, I didn't see this part of me at the time. I often wrote in my journal that I thought I wasn't being "productive." I felt as if I couldn't get my priorities together, while everyone else around me could. Jay would encourage me and tell me not to get down on myself. The problem was that Jay was frequently out to sea. The *Niagara Falls* would sail into the Indian Ocean and just hang out there. I felt alone at these times, without anyone to talk to. If my evals hadn't told me I was energetic and motivated, I would have had no idea.

Meanwhile, even from across the sea, Mama was still stressing me. From time to time, wherever I happened to be stationed, I'd send her gifts. I sent her a hand-crafted necklace from Egypt once with her name in English on one side and Arabic on the other. I sent her a blanket from Istanbul, a coffee pot from Italy, and other miscellaneous purchases I made along the way. I'd find out later that although she cherished the necklace, she'd often sell or return the other gifts for cash. Sometimes she'd tell me herself. "I didn't need that, Sharon," she'd say.

Soon enough, Jay and I transferred again. But now it was my turn to do sea duty. It was July, 1990 and, by then, the Navy was (finally) allowing women to serve on ships. I was assigned to the *USS McKee*, homeported at Naval Base Point Loma in San Diego. Jay got shore duty orders to SIMA, Shore Intermediate Maintenance Activity, at 32nd Street Naval Station, also in San Diego.

And that's when things started going south for Jay and me.

I became anxious about going out to sea. Not so much the sea part. It was the Navy, after all. It's what I'd signed up for. My anxiety came from the idea of again being separated from Jay. Unconsciously, I began to distance myself from him in the weeks leading up to my departure on the *McKee*. I felt as if our marriage was in trouble. I had it in my head that at any time, Jay might leave me for another woman. It was an ironic reaction to the situation; I was afraid of being separated from Jay, yet I began to separate myself from him. I knew it wasn't right, and I prayed about it often, prayed that I might be delivered from my worries and stress. And yet, in a moment of unwarranted mistrust, I gave Jay definitive ground rules. "We'll be in different time zones," I told him, "so keep the phone by the bed. And don't have nobody else in my bed!"

The *McKee* departed for the Persian Gulf. Along the way, I called Jay from piers in Hawaii, Singapore, Thailand, and Japan. But by the time we sailed into Jebel Ali, I'd get no answer at times when Jay should have been home. We were docked, the temperature was 117 degrees, the sand was blowing, and I couldn't reach my husband. Oh, and we were at war against Iraq. I was miserable. I even had Mama try to get in touch with Jay, but she didn't have any success either. One time I called and some dude answered the phone telling me Jay was at the store. It was obvious Jay had other people staying with him and I became certain that one of them had to have been a woman. I was done. I didn't give a damn who answered the phone.

Mama agreed. I never caught Jay in the act, but all signs pointed to cheating. In time, I would discover phone bills that showed calls to and from Inglewood. Mama told me to live my life, and that's what I did.

He was a fellow shipmate and his name was Michael.

Michael, too, was having problems at home and we gave each other what we both needed. Michael, already a friend, became my lover. We grew closer and what we shared was special. After returning from our six month cruise, I found myself late, believing I was pregnant. Michael and I loved each other, but we both knew we couldn't take things any further.

I never told Michael about the pregnancy, but I told Jay, who accepted the notion that I might be pregnant. He wanted to stick with the marriage and offered to raise the baby as his. In the end, me missing my period was due to stress. I hadn't been pregnant after all. But the marriage, in my eyes, was irreparable. After returning to port, and a few months of trying to hang with the marriage, I got my own apartment and then filed for divorce. Eventually, I would report to headquarters in NDW—Naval District Washington, DC. Jay followed me there. He was tired of West Coast duty and apparently had hopes of us getting back together. I'd lost all trust in him, though, and after my affair with Michael, I couldn't imagine how Jay could trust me either. At that point, my energies became even more focused on my career.

Years later, I would learn more about those people living with Jay and those missed phone calls and the mysterious calls to Inglewood. Jay needed money. We'd been living together on two incomes but when the *McKee* deployed, it hadn't occurred to me to make an allotment for Jay and send anything of my paycheck home. Jay never asked me to because he knew I'd been anxious and he didn't want to trouble me. Worse, I ran up phone bills calling him. Those calls from the piers at places like Hawaii and Singapore added up to over $1,200. I wouldn't stop talking and Jay never had the heart to tell me we needed to hang up, so he let me talk. Our car needed brakes, too. Jay had to keep taking duties. He even had to take in a roommate to make ends meet. The story was that his roommate was hustling weed and his connections were in Inglewood, thus the phone calls.

Jay had done what he felt he needed to do, but the marriage was now over. Looking back, it was inevitable. Jay was a good man. A good provider. But we were different people. He had an ideal in his mind for whom he wanted his wife to be and I was not that ideal. I'm not sure I was anybody's ideal. Whether he cheated on me or not, I didn't see it lasting, anyway. I must have sensed this all along, hence my quickness to believe he was cheating despite the lack of evidence. Nobody was at fault, really. But the marriage was over and Jay was now out of my life.

CHAPTER 8

ANCHORS AWEIGH

All along, I kept in touch with Daddy. We continued to write each other and he kept telling me that Jay better be treating me right. I didn't want to burden him with the news of the divorce, but I loved having Daddy's support and welcomed his encouragement. In one letter he wrote, "I know I haven't always been there for you, baby girl." Funny thing is I always felt as if he had been. All the times Daddy wasn't around, I felt his presence. I knew he loved me and thought of me often.

After Daddy had fallen down the basement stairs at Jerry's house, he had gone to a physical rehabilitation facility in Hanover, Indiana, about an hour away. I don't know why my brother didn't choose a closer place. He visited Daddy infrequently. Daddy explained in one of his letters to me that Jerry didn't come very often because he was afraid it would mess with the Medicaid coverage of the rehabilitation, as if somehow it would become apparent that Daddy had people who could take care of him and therefore didn't need the rehab. I couldn't believe the excuse my brother had made. Years later, I would pick up Daddy from a nursing home for a visit and Mama would say the exact same thing to me. "Sharon, you don't need to be getting JW from the nursing home. They gonna think you can take care of him." I saw where my brother got the excuse from. Just like Mama.

Daddy spent about a year or so in Hanover and then came back to Jerry's place. He wrote me soon afterward, saying, "I'm going to tell you, before you hear it from your mama, that I've been home for a few days and I admit I've had a few 'smiles.' But I'm going to make you proud of me, baby girl!" Just like Daddy. I might have lost one man in my life, but I'd always have my Daddy.

———⋅⋙⋅———

The *USS McKee*, hull number AS-41 and home-ported in Point Loma, San Diego, was a ship that never went anywhere. That's what everybody said, anyway. They called her "Building 41" as though she were a permanent, immovable structure. But right about the time I reported to her for sea duty, a little something was going on over in the Persian Gulf, namely, Operation Desert Storm, which came to be known as the Gulf War.

In early August of 1990, Iraq invaded neighboring Kuwait. This was just a week or so after my transfer to the *McKee*. Months of failed diplomacy would follow and, eventually, with Iraq within striking distance of Saudi oil fields, the US lead a coalition of nations against Iraq in January of 1991. In the end, Iraq wasn't much of an opponent. The war lasted one month, one week, and four days.

During that time, the *McKee* was dual-designated—supply and repair. She served as a supply tender for submarines and destroyers while taking repair orders from several ships in the Gulf and delivering admirably. She was referred to as the "*McKee* Naval Shipyard," and even displayed a banner with this title. A couple ships, the *Princeton* and the *Tripoli*, had taken direct hits and we supported a few displaced sailors with room and board. After her deployment, the *McKee* would be awarded her second Meritorious Unit Commendation.

I reported to the ship in September of '90, before hostilities started. By then, after having done ten years of shore duty, I'd almost forgotten the protocol from boot camp for boarding a Navy vessel. I was nervous walking up the long shaky gangway to the quarterdeck. Once there, the officer of the deck (OOD) reminded me that I needed to salute the ensign (flag), salute the OOD, and request permission to come aboard. When permission was granted, I was escorted to meet my supervisor.

The *McKee* was 23,000 tons and was 645-feet long, with a beam of 85 feet and a draft of 26 feet. She had a top speed of 20 knots and a crew that numbered 1,400. I came aboard as one of the leading petty officers, responsible for the operation and sanitation of the general mess. We wouldn't sail for the Persian Gulf until January, which gave me a few months to get used to the ship that would be my home for a while. In fact, I got busy learning all about the ship and I earned my ESWS pin—Enlisted Surface Warfare Specialist. It wasn't a required qualification, but I wanted to show that I was there to excel and lead. Earning the pin required knowing all aspects of the *McKee*, including all the specifications and all of the flags of the ship, from Alpha to Zebra. It meant going to each division—communications, engineering, medical, navigation, weapons, everything—and learning their roles and getting a qualified technical expert, LPO, or CPO to sign off. It was time-consuming and the accomplishment wasn't easy for someone like me in food service where my days as a cook could be twelve or fourteen hours long.

Everyone had to learn about my division, too. In fact, all the newly reporting junior personnel who were assigned to the ship had to spend their first nine-ty days in the galley with me before reporting to their respective divisions. It was shipboard protocol for E3 sailors and below to learn the intricacies of the ship's food service division, to make them respect the im-portance of what we did and the hard work that took place to make sure that everyone on board the ship was well fed. This meant that in addition to my own food service people, I had a revolving door of junior newbies. It also meant that everyone on board, at one point or another, worked for me. Over time, I got a reputation. Senior sailors would tell junior sailors, "You're going to work for Chief Jordan? *Good luck.*"

There were ships that had already been in the Per-sian Gulf, but ours was the first to leave after the war had started, which meant a lot of fanfare on our way out. Our last port of call before arriving at Jebel Ali was in Singapore. Between Singapore and Jebel Ali, we crossed the equator, a milestone that's been cele-brated by sailors since the old-time sailing days. When you cross, you transform from a slimy "pollywog" to a "shellback." The ceremony for new shellbacks comes with initiation rites that include all kinds of nasty things, mostly involving forms of humiliation. On the *McKee*, sailors had to wear their underwear over their pants, wear their pants and boots backwards while crawling on their hands and knees, get dunked, eat some ugly foods (which was my food service's job), and undergo similar indignities, including sucking the cherry out of "King Neptune's belly," the belly button of the fattest sailor on the ship. The ceremony was supposedly a test of seaworthiness. We all had a good time, even those of us suffering the humiliations.

When I'd come aboard the *McKee*, I'd been anxious about going out to sea, mostly because I'd be separated from Jay, but there were all the other little concerns, too, like seasickness or just being stuck on a ship and not being able to walk on firm ground for weeks at a time. But once aboard, I soon got my sea legs and found that I had too much to do to be worried about anything beyond my duties. Plus, I had to deal with a bunch of subordinates that I didn't know, which wasn't easy. There were a couple of cliques of young female sailors that hung together, some of whom I had to keep on top of constantly about their long nails, fingernail polish, makeup, and mostly about their head-swaying, eye-rolling attitudes. I also had a bunch of guys that didn't especially care to be working for a woman, or *with* a woman, for that matter. It was a ship full of strangers. It wasn't part of my job description, but even if it had been, it wasn't easy to make friends.

The *McKee* was one of the first ships to integrate women, but ninety percent of the sailors and officers were men. Not surprisingly, there was some sexism on board. Besides the men who resented working under female leadership, there was our division officer, Warrant Officer McGill, a bald guy who was always sucking up to his superiors and who had a good-old-boy network firmly in place. Even though working in the officers' mess was for those juniors who had proven themselves stellar performers, McGill once assigned a young, inexperienced female sailor to the officers' mess. The only qualification this girl had was her ability to bat her eyes to get what she wanted, especially from McGill. The girl was untouchable. Meanwhile, the general mess cooks had to bust their butts down in the main galley, cleaning the grills and carrying out all the other tedious food service duties.

There were other examples of sexism, too, as well as examples of racism, though, like McGill's good-old-boy network, nothing overt. For my part, I blocked most of it out and kept it moving, though I made it a point not to take any crap from anyone, male or female, black or white. I took some satisfaction in disrupting some networks—cliques that I was too independent to feel any connection with. I hadn't left my anger back on land, and I told off a few superiors from time to time, along with some peers. But I did my job and I did it well. The people whose opinions really mattered were taking note.

Still, it was hard for me. Part of the problem may have been that I was still relatively young. When I came on board, I was what was called an early promote. Maybe I'd achieved first class too quickly for everyone, seven years when the norm was somewhere around eight to ten. I could have done it in six, I'll bet, had it not been for the lieutenant who'd lowered my marks in personal behavior. Apparently, my rate of progress led to the misperception of me as arrogant and self-important, and it seemed like I was always fighting somebody, always in conflict with my counterparts. I even acquired a rival at the time. MS1 Nancy Wood was a leading petty officer who pretty much had her way with the good-old-boy network, yet she still resented me. I found myself in competition but it wasn't me who'd wanted to compete. I just wanted to do my job.

Some nights I'd go out on the weather deck and look out over the moonlit water, and everything would be all right again. I'd gather a sense of peace and most of those nights I felt as if I could have stayed out there forever. I kept the faith in those moments and I came to think of the Pacific Ocean and the Arabian Peninsula as my "full armor of God."

Then it would be back down below. To all the craziness.

Sometimes my frustration would come out a little intensely, especially with my subordinates. At the start of the day, each division officer or leading chief would hold muster with his or her people in their respective areas, issuing the POD—plan of the day. The other divisions would finish and the sailors would be walking to their departments or stations, but my musters sometimes went into overtime. Sailors would often pass through my mess decks and hear me kicking some royal ass, dressing down my people for something stupid they'd done or some act of total incompetence. You could hear the sailors snickering as they went by while I'd make someone come front and center and stand at attention while I raked them over the coals. The funny thing is, even when I tried to be more discreet, pulling a subordinate into my office to yell at them, it didn't help. People outside the office could hear me anyway.

And so I wasn't always Miss Popularity, but I did eventually manage to make a good friend. Nada Cox was in food service, too, a fellow first-class, a fellow black woman, and, like Pam, another mellow counterweight. She had to put up with the same stuff I had to put up with—sexism, racism, general rebelliousness on the part of our subordinates, and the good-old-boy network. But Nada was from Louisiana and some of the sailors were unbelievably fearful that MS1 Cox would put some kind of Voodoo curse on them. They didn't mess with Nada.

This, of course, was around the time I was struggling with my marriage. Nada was having problems with her husband, too, something else we both had in common. She became the only person on the ship I felt comfortable talking to. We stayed friends, even after the ship made its way back to San Diego. One night after leaving the ship, we went to Spanish Landing and drank so much our husbands had to come and get us. Nada and I remain close friends to this day. Sisters, really.

Upon pulling into port from the Persian Gulf, the chiefs results had come in. I'd been selected for Chief Petty Officer. MS1 Woods received a NAM, Navy Achievement Medal, during the command ceremony on the flight deck. But I'd been selected. The head shakers with their attitudes throttled back a bit. I'd been recommended for CPO based on "sustained superior performance" and I was ranked first of seven first-class petty officers assigned to the food service division. I was described as a "proven manager and leader of boundless potential."

Soon after, I was pinned with anchors on my collars.

I remained on the *McKee* until June of 1993, though of course the war was over. We would continue to go out for sea trials for a couple of weeks at a time. The captain of the McKee during those days was Captain Wynn Harding. Captain Harding had a calm, soft-spoken demeanor and was very encouraging to me. Often, when back at Point Loma, the captain would throw parties at his house for the *McKee* officers and their wives, and Nada and I would do the food, although Nada was more the culinary specialist than I was, typically preparing the fancier stuff. I was more or less a boil-the-water, flip-the-burgers kind of cook. Nada and I got to know the captain's wife, Patty, at these get-togethers and she was as down to earth and just as kind as the skipper.

My supply officer at the time was Commander Ronald Popp. He had the same demeanor as Captain Harding and was just as encouraging. I enjoyed serving under both Captain Harding and Commander Popp and I could not have had a better first ship to serve on. On my final eval on the *McKee*, Captain Harding wrote that I was "hard charging and versatile...a superb leader of the toughest division on the ship." At one point, I had volunteered for the damage control training team. Captain Harding wrote, "A mess management specialist running flying squad and mainspace fire drills. I was awed!" Then he handwrote on the eval, "A superstar who will be deeply missed on *McKee*. Promote ASAP."

I would keep in touch with Captain Harding for years, even visiting with him and his wife. I'd keep in touch with Commander Popp, too, who would write to me and always wish me well. A couple of years after my McKee service, Captain Harding would write a slammin' recommendation for me. "She is the leader against whom others can be measured. You will not find one better."

My sea duty was finally over, with all its ups and downs. Back on land there was Michael, my false pregnancy, and my break-up with Jay. Sometimes it seemed the only time everything was under my control, even with the conflicts I might have had with certain shipmates, was when I was on duty. No wonder I thrived on it so much. My next assignment? Headquarters, Naval District, Washington, DC.

CHAPTER 9

OUR NATION'S CAPITAL

After my service on the *McKee*, I had an opportunity for flag staff duty. Flag staff duty means working for a senior staff member or Admiral, or even someone like the president. It's prestigious. It can be demanding, depending on the specific assignment, but it can also help propel your career. I had taken private mess school by then, which was geared toward flag staff duty where you're cooking for commanding officers, admirals, and visiting dignitaries.

I was assigned to the Visiting Flag Quarters (VFQ), Naval District Washington, DC—NDW. This was more or less a bed and breakfast for distinguished visitors of the chief of naval operations, like ambassadors and prime ministers and other visiting bigwigs. To be considered for such elite duty, I was required to send a videotaped interview, conducted by my supply officer, Commander Popp. He asked me questions like why I would want such a duty and what I hoped to accomplish. For the VFQ, I guess the Navy not only needed to know what my answers were, but they needed to know how articulate I was. Apparently, appearance also counted; in addition to the tape, I had to supply photos of me in uniform, I assume as witness to my stature and military bearing.

Apparently, the manager, a civilian lady named Bev Upperman, liked what she saw and selected me for duty. I moved to DC and reported as the VFQ Assistant Manager. My first impressions of Upperman were not good and my first impressions were correct. Upperman turned out to be a snooty, power hungry, big-busted woman who talked down to me. She loved being in charge and I found out very quickly that everything had to be done her way. This worked out well for the assistant I was replacing—Petty Officer First Class Roy Clemmons, a little black Mini-Me who was a real butt-snorkeler. My first day there, he worked my nerves saying, "Yes, Ms. Upperman," and "Right, Ms. Upperman." I'd do something a certain way and he'd say, "Oh, no, that's not going to work at all. Ms. Upperman is *not* going to go for that."

Immediately I suspected I'd made a mistake taking this duty and, needless to say, it didn't work out quite so well for me as it had for Clemmons. I needed some latitude to do things the way I felt they needed to be done. But creativity was discouraged. "We have a way of doing things here," was Ms. Upperman's mantra. Worse, I had two junior MSs under me and I wasn't even allowed to direct them. They were cooks, working for me, but only took their orders from Upperman.

And Upperman preferred it if I stayed behind the scenes, rather than interact with the visiting dignitaries. "Chief, you can just leave the keys for the Admiral," she'd say in a snarly Nurse Ratched voice. "I know what he wants. You don't have to be here when he arrives." Upperman wanted me to stick to the back room or the kitchen. One time she directed me to speak with the horticulturist about the exterior flowers in anticipation of an Admiral's visit. I barely knew what a horticulturist was. I told Upperman that I didn't join the Navy to work with no damn flower doctor. Upperman wasn't shy about reminding me of the many others who'd been interviewed for my position, implying that I was fortunate to be there working for her. I disliked her tone and the smirk she always had on her face reminded me of Mama and the way she'd convey disappointment in me.

It was supposed to be a two-year tour, and even though it seemed like two years, I could tough it out under Upperman for only ten months. I went to see the commandant, Admiral Edward Moore. As it happened, I had seen him often at the Navy Yard Chapel on Sundays where a lot of district staff attended service, including the chief of naval operations, Admiral Frank Kelso, as well as other high-ranking people from the Pentagon. I didn't sweat who attended. I was there because it was Sunday and back then, on Sundays, I went to church. Anyway, one Sunday, I approached Admiral Moore and asked if I could come see him.

"I don't think I'm doing a very good job at the VFQ, Admiral," I said.

"Come see me anytime, Chief," he told me.

I ran the request and told Upperman, who said, "I know you don't like it here, Chief, but the Admiral isn't going to see you over this nonsense." But of course he did. And in the Admiral's office, I told him my job wasn't at all fulfilling. I needed more of a challenge and wanted more responsibility. Working for Upperman, without any ability to do anything as I saw fit, made it feel as if I were just a walking, empty uniform. What was the point of making Chief? Upperman was working my nerves, I told the Admiral. I knew that the Navy was getting ready to start a new command at Bolling Air Force Base right there in DC. They were going to call it Naval Station Anacostia. Today it's known as Joint Base Anacostia-Bolling. "Maybe I can serve over there," I said. Admiral Moore thought it was a good idea and that was it for me at the VFQ. I left without Ms. Upperman saying so much as goodbye, good luck, or glad to see you go. That was the leadership I'd been under?

At Bolling, I was the new BEQ manager, housing Navy personnel in Blanchard Barracks, a building that was split between Navy and Air Force personnel. I also managed the Ceremonial Honor Guard barracks. These are the guys who represent the Navy in presidential ceremonies, or Navy or joint armed forces ceremonies, in and around DC. They do parades, state funeral processions, and a myriad of other high-visibility functions, including every Navy funeral service conducted in Arlington National Cemetery. Despite their ceremonial seriousness, around the barracks these guys were funny and mischievous and always liked trying to get a rise out of me. Prim and proper in their uniforms, some of them were surprisingly sloppy, too. Just before I would eventually transfer, they'd present me with an honorary ceremonial honor guard jacket. On one side of the front it was embroidered with "Navy's Finest" and on the other side, "BQ Mgr. CJ" for Chief Jordan. I loved those guys. And I still have that jacket.

I housed transient Navy personnel, too—"general detachment" or "GENDET" personnel, sailors who were on their way elsewhere, some getting processed out, some in a limited-duty status, maybe recovering from illness or injury, or even some who were awaiting disciplinary action for something they'd done. I had four MS's who worked for me permanently, but the limited-duty personnel worked for me too, even though some of them were there because they didn't care to work in the first place. But as long as they lived in my barracks and were able-bodied, they worked. They did maintenance, groundskeeping, and even office work. It wasn't always easy to work with these sailors, but I was lenient and tried to make things fun for them, figuring they'd appreciate not having a chief who micromanaged. And even with nonstop rotation of GENDET personnel, the work always managed to get done.

Between the sailors in Blanchard Barracks and the GENDETS, I housed about 380 sailors. For myself, I rented an apartment right off Indian Head Highway in Fort Washington, Maryland, close to the front gate of the base. One day, I conducted a barracks inspection and saw the name Jordan on my resident roster. When I entered the room it was immaculate. I knew Jay was a neat freak, but I couldn't imagine that it was him. It just couldn't be. But it was. One of my 380 residents was my ex-husband.

Jay had come to DC supposedly because he was tired of the West Coast. But he also admitted that he was hoping we'd reunite. He'd reported for duty at Naval Station Security, Washington, DC. Jay and I started hanging out with each other, but not as a couple. To me, it was more like having a family member around to do things with. Jay, of course, wanted more, but I could no longer commit to Jay. To make matters worse, I fooled around with a good friend of his, although I guess he couldn't have been that much of a friend. Anthony had two young kids he was raising by himself and I just wanted to help. One thing led to another and I ended up sleeping with Anthony. It only happened once and I realized immediately it was a mistake, just like with Rasheeno all those years before. In my regret, I told Jay about it. He was hurt. We'd both hurt him.

My service continued going well, even with all the personal drama in the background. A highlight was being chosen for the Military Mass Choir. I auditioned on tape, singing acapella "The Star Spangled Banner" and sending in the cassette. It was an honor to be selected. Among other venues, we'd sing in the White House, typically for tourists or maybe a foreign dignitary. I never had a chance to meet the primary occupant of the house, unfortunately, but it was exciting just the same.

I did a few of the tourist things while in DC. I toured the Treasury Building, hit up a few museums, and saw the Vietnam Veterans Memorial. One place I couldn't resist visiting was Rock Creek Park. I remembered singing "Rock Creek Park," an old disco song by the Blackbyrds, in my basement with Stephanie during our pretend talent shows. I didn't know the park actually existed until I was driving along one day and saw a sign for it on the parkway.

Mama came to visit me in DC. We saw some of the sights. She said she was proud of me, but then also had to mention that she thought I was drinking too much. Her pattern of manipulation was still going strong. Meanwhile, for whatever reason, I kept trying to please her. Maybe that's just the way it is with a person's mother. Or maybe her comment long ago—back when I was just a teenager sitting at the department of corrections downtown after I got busted for stealing from the Kroger's—had never left me. "Leave her there," she had said. "Just leave her in there."

At one point, I filled out all the paperwork necessary to make Mama a military dependent. This came with a long list of benefits. I explained everything to Mama well beforehand but when the Navy sent the paperwork to her to sign, she wrote on it, "I am not dependent on my daughter!" and sent it back. So there I was, still trying to support her on my own.

I learned later that, back home, Mama would tell people how proud she was of me. She'd brag about me. But to me, she rarely said anything of the sort. If she did admit to being proud of me, it seemed like she was saying it out of obligation, and she would phrase it to make it sound as if she were somehow doing me a favor. "I told so-and-so the other day how proud of you I am," she'd tell me, as if she was expecting gratitude for bragging about me.

I wrote to Daddy often, sending him t-shirts and Navy ball caps with my command's name on them. I would see him on leave sometimes when I'd make the nine-hour drive back to Louisville. Of course Mama never stopped criticizing him around me, constantly making sarcastic comments. Being with Daddy and out of the continued negativity of Mama's house was always a blessing. But Daddy was still drinking pretty heavily and had developed gout. His feet were so swollen that he had to rip holes in his sneakers. He'd grown a long scraggly beard, too. But we'd always sit out on the porch of Jerry's house and have a few "smiles" together.

One time, at the nursing home, I was giving him a mani-pedi, and I asked, "Daddy, do you think I'm pretty?"

"You ain't ugly," he said.

"You don't want to say I'm pretty; you think it'll go to my head, huh?"

Daddy nodded. He let some time lapse, keeping focused on the TV show he'd been watching. Finally, he looked over at me and said, "You know you're pretty." Daddy always made me feel better.

One day in 1994, they found him walking around the backyard completely lost. He'd developed dementia. Not long after that, Daddy had to be placed in a nursing home.

Back at Anacostia, I submitted my second application package for LDO, Limited Duty Officer. While on the *McKee*, I had submitted my first, with no luck in getting selected. LDOs are enlisted personnel selected to become commissioned officers because of their high skill level and achievements. Back in Guam, I had started compiling all my accolades, schooling, volunteering, letters of achievement, character references, and the like. I'd written letters to Congressmen, and councilmen. Now I sent letters to a few of my Admiral friends, the Kentucky attorney general, inspectors, COs, and others asking for letters of recommendation. As it happened, the Kentucky AG, David Armstrong, was the one who signed off on my completion of the diversion program I'd entered way back when. He was happy to send a recommendation, knowing I'd chosen the right path.

I even asked Admiral Kelso, sending him a package of my achievements and evaluations. I just threw that one out there, knowing it wouldn't get very far, but I had met the Admiral at the Navy Yard Chapel and I guess I was just looking for a chance to show off to him. To his credit, he was kind enough to write back, saying that he wasn't in a position to endorse my application, but that I had a fine record and he appreciated what I had done "for our Navy." The voice of approval meant a lot to me.

I sent letters to both Kentucky senators, Ron Mazzoli, and Mitch McConnell. McConnell didn't give
me a recommendation, but Senator Mazzoli did. It
was simple and to the point: "I would appreciate
appropriate consideration." I liked that. I kept in
touch with the senator for years afterward, even after
I'd retired. I also contacted the president of the International Food Service Executives Association, Ed
Manley. IFSEA sponsored the inspectors who came
around to inspect the galleys/EDFs Navy-wide. Ed
gave me a recommendation and also showed me how
to become a certified food executive.

LDO wasn't easy. Ultimately, it would take me not
two, but three attempts to achieve it.

Meanwhile, I found myself chafing against the orders of yet another superior. Lieutenant JG (Junior
Grade) Henderson became my new division officer
and proceeded to undermine me in every way. Henderson was as cutthroat as they came. And, like Upperman, felt as if she knew everything. But, as Daddy
was fond of saying, she didn't know shit from apple
butter. My crew and I couldn't do our jobs effectively
because of her micromanaging.

To me, it seemed as if she didn't trust me. If we
worked with another command, she'd be sure to talk
directly to the chief of the other command. But that
wasn't her job. Chiefs talk to other chiefs. But she had
to make the initial approach, to let everyone think she

was in charge. It was not unlike how Upperman kept me from interacting with visiting dignitaries. It was not only micromanaging, it was disrespectful. It was a slap in the face. And it didn't help my state of mind to know that I was smarter than she was.

The MAIT team—the Navy's Management, Assistance, and Inspection Team—came in to inspect and picked up on the dynamics right away. In particular, during the debrief to the CO, they reported on how knowledgeable and impressed they were with me and my LPO MS1 Ronnell Hopkins. They didn't mention Henderson.

The situation fed into my anxiety and depression. Worse, I made a trip home on leave and had to deal with Mama. True to form, she spoke badly of Daddy to me. There Daddy was in a nursing home and Mama couldn't stop ragging on him. Plus, I was seeing friends and trying to relax, having some drinks here and there because I never did much relaxing at Anacostia, or at any of my commands. I was always too focused on trying to do my job. But I was a sailor. And on leave, I would sometimes drink like a sailor. To hear Mama tell it, you'd think I was a full-blown raging alcoholic. She even asked Daddy to talk to me about it. Daddy told me not to give it a second thought. "Hell, I'm the pisshead of the family," he told me, "not you."

I went to Shawnee park and wrote all my thoughts about Mama down on paper. Then I went to her and spoke to her about her negativity, about her hurtful comments, about the little manipulations. She acted bewildered. "That's just your imagination, Sharon," she said.

Back at Anacostia, I decided I was ready to seek some counseling. Unlike earlier in my career when I hadn't wanted to talk to someone about my emotional well-being, this time I sought out the counsel of the base chaplain, Commander Judy Cadenhead. It was good to open up to someone and Cadenhead provided a lot of help. At one point she suggested that maybe I should go to medical; perhaps they could prescribe something for my anxiety. But I didn't want my mind muddled.

For me, it was time to get out of Anacostia. Senior Chief Navy Counselor Drexel Mitchell, or "Mitch," as everyone called him, counseled me on going back to sea duty. We had met at the Navy Annex in Arlington. I had been a chief for over a year and Mitch was my first mentor. He had schooled me on how to write and build my evaluations, especially while preparing my LDO application. He counseled me on much more, too. He was also a minister and I often thought the Navy was not his first, but his second job because of his devout faith in God. He was always reminding me of the importance of faith in God and in myself. Whenever I was struggling with something, Mitch would say, "All right, Chief Jordan, where's your faith? How 'bout we pray about it?" Mitch's guidance propelled my faith in God and in myself. To this day we remain friends. Mitch retired as a master chief, obtained his doctorate, and is now a presiding elder in the Fourth District CME church in Texas.

Otherwise, I didn't make a lot of friends during my time in DC, even though I knew a lot of people. Nada was stationed not far away at Fort Meade, close to BWI, and she came to visit me and I'd go see her too. I was either too busy, or maybe I just wasn't in a place where, emotionally, I felt as though I could trust many people.

At any rate, I told Henderson's obnoxious butt, "I'd rather go to sea and get hazardous duty pay than spend another day working for you."

My next duty: The *USS La Salle*.

Chapter 10

My Finest Hour

After telling Henderson I'd had enough of her, I submitted my request to go back to sea. I had a few options to choose from. One was serving at United States Naval Support Activity (NSA) Souda Bay at the Hellenic Air Force Base on the northwest coast of the Greek island of Crete. Another was serving on the oiler *USS Butte*, homeported at Naval Weapons Station Earle in New Jersey. I was also offered presidential duty—working at the White House. A lot of gung-ho sailors would have jumped at the chance to work at the White House. Me, I saw it as just another Visiting Flag Quarters sort of gig, only more so. Lots of supervision and meddling, lots of nit-picking, and lots of butt snorkeling. I didn't join the Navy to be a butt-snorkeler.

I seriously considered the *Butte*, because I still had family in New Jersey—Aunt Ann and my cousins

Cookie and Flip. New Jersey was where I first saw the ocean, the location to where I had taken my first plane ride, the place that had sparked my interest in traveling. Crete, beautiful and exotic, seemed promising, too, but it wasn't sea duty. I wanted to serve on a ship again. And that's where the *USS LaSalle* came into the picture, the best of both worlds—an exotic location, plus sea duty. The *LaSalle* was homeported in Gaeta, Italy, a picturesque seaside resort town about halfway between Rome and Naples. And it was the flagship for the commander of the US Sixth Fleet. I submitted my 1306 request and off to Italy I went.

The *LaSalle* was a 13,900-ton vessel, 521 feet in length with an 84-foot beam and a 21-foot draft. Four-hundred and ninety enlisted personnel served aboard her along with 21 officers. The Sixth Fleet consisted of some forty ships, all under the command of Vice Admiral Donald Pilling, and the *LaSalle*, as the fleet's flagship, was his ship. That didn't mean that the Admiral was always aboard. In fact, most of the time, he was represented on board by his chief of staff. Meanwhile, the one in actual day-to-day charge of the ship was the captain, Captain Mark Milliken at the time I came aboard. What this meant was that there were LaSalle personnel on board, like me, and then there were the members of the Sixth Fleet staff. You knew these guys when you saw them. They were always squared away, uniforms always perfect. They could be snooty, too, and it appeared to me like they thought they were just a little better than us on the LaSalle. Of course they'd better have been; they were the Admiral's select.

As for the LaSalle people, I had no complaints. I didn't find nearly the same amount of jealousy and back stabbings that I'd experienced on the McKee. My direct supervisor was Senior Chief Cipriano Lontoc. Senior Chief was cool. He was a petite fellow, mild mannered, and he let me do my job. Quite the opposite of what I'd experienced at VFQ Naval District Washington and Naval Station Anacostia, in other words. Senior Chief was an insane stickler for cleanliness, though. A sanitation guru. We called him the mad scientist because this guy would climb onto the grill and crawl into the Gaylord to inspect it. But that was okay with me. Senior Chief Cipriano Lontoc became my new role model.

I had great respect for the captains I served under, too, during my time on the *LaSalle*. After Milliken, there was Captain Mark Caren and then Captain Bruce Clingan. All of them were top-notch good guys, highly respectable and respected. Today Captain Milliken is a retired rear Admiral and Captain Clingan a retired vice Admiral.

I came aboard as the leading Chief Petty Officer of the food service division, S-2. We had a motto: "S-2 Can Do." I soon qualified for a lot of additional duties, including shore patrol when we were in port, just like the guys who had broken up my fight in Puerto Rico. I also qualified for Junior Officer of the Watch. The JOOW stands watch on the bridge with the OOD—Officer Of the Deck. I learned how to drive the ship and learned everyone's role on the bridge. Meanwhile, all the time I was qualifying, I was still standing my watches and running all three messes—the chief's mess, the officers' mess, the crew's mess.

The demands of Sixth Fleet were constant. As my responsibilities became heavier, the more difficult it became for me to manage my not-yet-diagnosed ADHD. But I had help. My LPO, MS1 Margaret Pinzone, was a logistical genius. Short, sharp, and with sleeves always rolled up, she had my back, continually informing me of what was going on and what needed to be done and when. I even began to wonder if she somehow picked up on my imposter syndrome. She was always a step ahead, making sure I was prepared and never in danger of dropping the ball. It was an LPO's job to do that, but I took it personally that she had my back, helping me to shine. My two galley petty-officers-in-charge also helped keep things on track. MS1 Bentham Kline was a top-notch baker and MS2 Gregory Harvey was a top-notch cook. Pinzone, Kline, and Harvey would say, "We got you, Chief," and all I'd have to say is, "Aye Aye."

The imposter syndrome is something I wouldn't realize I had until much later in life. For the most part, I came across as something of a badass. I knew what I was doing, I didn't have a lot of patience with people who weren't doing their jobs right, and I wasn't afraid to speak out. But was I a badass? It seems looking back that I was a badass because being a badass worked for me at the time. I can't say with any certainty that it's who I really was.

If anything, I was *masking*, a psychological term that means just what it says—you hide or "mask" your natural personality to conform to the expectations of others. You try to be the person you think they want or expect you to be. Later, I would learn that this is not uncommon for people living with ADHD. It's a coping mechanism we employ because of our fear of being discovered that we're somehow different. Often it's learned in childhood. We're told repeatedly to "pay attention" and even criticized for our apparent lack of focus. And so in front of others, we fake it. We pretend we're not who we really are and it can be exhausting. I didn't know any of this at the time, of course.

One thing I did know was that I loved the *LaSalle*. The entire crew felt the same way. We were united. And the ship didn't just rest in port. We went everywhere: different ports in Italy, Greece, Slovenia, Croatia, Turkey, France, Spain, Israel, Egypt, Bulgaria, Romania, Ukraine, even Russia. In all, we made port at twenty-five cities in twenty different countries. The Navy kept its promise and showed me the world. And every time we'd make port, I'd make sure to buy a little something—suede boots in Slovenia, marble bookends in Barcelona, whatever I could find that was locally crafted.

Sixth Fleet took great pride in entertaining foreign dignitaries. As flagship, we'd pull into their port, bring them on board, and "smooge" them—entertain them with a big spread of food and drinks. At times, we'd allow small groups to come aboard. I met a young girl from Czechoslovakia once named Latizia, about twelve years old. We befriended each other and kept in touch. She wrote to me that she loved Michael Jackson.

But for all our travels, the place I ended up loving the most was our homeport. Gaeta was small and charming with cobblestone streets. The Italian folk were always courteous and hospitable, and they seemed genuinely appreciative of the US naval presence. There was a bar named Rendezvous right off the long pier where everybody hung out and the staff seemed to know every sailor's name. The people of the town did their best to understand our English, just as we would try our best to understand their Italian. Most conversations included a lot of hand gesturing. I tried to learn the language but could never keep still long enough to study. Nonetheless, the locals would flatter me by claiming I was *molto gentile*—very nice. Some took to calling me *Capitano*, despite the fact that I was nowhere near being a captain.

I decided, when we were ported, to live off-ship. There was a lot of paperwork involved to rent an apartment, but I found a beautiful little place on *Via Independenza* with a cool landlord named Vincenzo. Vinny, bald on top with a skirt of white hair around his head, was a big guy with a big belly. And with Vinny, everything was always *"no problema."* I loved my apartment, but in Gaeta, I learned to get out. Most days, when not on duty, you could find me in a café or trattoria, or maybe sitting in the piazza on the waterfront, in view of the *LaSalle*, watching the people go by, journaling, and enjoying the Mediterranean breeze.

In time, I'd learn more about Vinny than I wanted to know. Once, knowing I was heading out to sea, I asked him to take care of my Nissan pickup, even giving him a letter authorizing him to drive it if he wanted. He was pulled over one day and had to show the *polizia* the letter. But as it turned out, the police were interested in him for more than just the pickup. Who would have guessed my Italian friend was affiliated with the Camorra crime family? This hadn't been Vinnie's first rodeo with being arrested. He'd been arrested before. In fact, two of his brothers were doing life in prison for racketeering, narcotics, and homicides. The captain received a message on board the ship stating that my pickup had been impounded. NCIS even questioned me, but of course I was clueless. As far as I know, the *polizia* still have my pickup. I never saw it again.

Meanwhile, on the *LaSalle*, I was exploring the world, making great memories, and lasting friendships in the process. We were a tight group. We saw a lot of the world together. We suffered our share of tragedies, too. Four junior guys who had all worked under me at one time or another, were coming back from Naples one night when a car hit them head on. Seaman Apprentice Christopher Carter, Fireman Recruit Stanley Ford, Jr., Radioman Seaman Recruit Rashad Litton, and Yeoman Seaman Apprentice Anthony Watkins. All four were killed. And then we lost another sailor in a separate car wreck a few months afterward—Fireman Michael Fleming.

Then one day, I took the duty of a newly reported master chief so that he could play in the chief's basketball game that was scheduled for that evening. We had been shooting the breeze in the chief's lounge just the day before. In fact, Master Chief Mike Holmes would frequently hang out with us in the chief's lounge. On the day we talked, he spoke about his wife and family and their experience traveling to Italy. MC Holmes was a stand-up guy and he'd become an immediate role model for me. His death might have been the most shocking to me. During the basketball game, he collapsed on the court and died.

The crew came together after the deaths, each of us trying to lift the others up. One of the four from the first car accident, Radioman Seaman Recruit Litton, had been a Sixth Fleet sailor and after that I could feel us bonding as one.

Of course I had a few anti-social issues with some of my shipmates. My supply officer and my division officer were both pricks. Supply Officer (SUPPO) Mike Lucas didn't much care for me at all, showing favoritism to others, especially to another female chief. Every time we'd pull back into Gaeta, this chick would be off the watch bill. I was told it was because she had family there. What if I'd had family there? How would that have worked? At one point, I'd had enough and I went down to Lucas's office and said, "Look, SUPPO, I don't know if it's because I'm black, I'm a woman, or I've got this gap in my teeth, but I want to know why every time we pull into home port, Petrucci's off the watch bill. What's the deal with that?"

"Chief," he began, "You're out of l—"

"No, I ain't," I interrupted. "I ain't out of line. All I'm doing is asking a question. Every time we pull back into port, I've got the duty. Now—black, woman, gap. Which one is it? I just came in here to find out, because this has been going on ever since I reported on board this ship!" I didn't stick around for an answer.

I walked out of his office. Things didn't change and I didn't expect they would, but at least he knew where I stood.

My superiors, on the other hand, the people who mattered, treated me with respect. I got called out of my rack one day because Executive Officers Shakespeare, who was soon to leave the *LaSalle*, and Singleton, who was the new XO, wanted to see me. "MSC Jordan report to the XO's office ASAP," came the announcement over the 1MC, the ship's public address system. Being summoned to the XO's office was usually trouble, especially for the S-2 division. It seemed I was always being called in for something. But in Commander Singleton's office that day, they told me I'd been selected for warrant officer. It was the only food-service-warrant slot open that year and I had been chosen. It was an amazing honor. The funny thing was, The XO had called my supply and division officers in for the official announcement too, per Navy protocol. They stood, put on fake airs, and shook my hand to offer their congratulations. So I put on my fake face and accepted the handshakes, forcing myself not to say aloud what I was thinking: *How do you like me now, assholes?*

Soon afterward, I was selected for another prestigious position. Senior Chief E.M. David came aboard one day to tell me I'd been chosen to be a Ney inspector for Commander Fleet Air Mediterranean. The

Captain Edward F. Ney Award, an award program established by IFSEA and the Secretary of the Navy for food-service excellence, was given to the very best galleys as determined by certified food inspectors. That year, for the general messes of Navy installations in Souda Bay, Crete; Rota, Spain; and Sigonella and Naples, Italy, I was to be lead inspector. It was another amazing honor. Inspectors were esteemed, even feared. I couldn't believe I was going to be one.

Senior Chief David had twenty-four years in the Navy and he trained me on everything, including how to prepare the inspection write-ups. We inspected for quality of food, administration, management, facilities, safety, training, and sanitation. Over a two-week period, we flew from base to base doing inspections. I felt like royalty. It was a whirlwind couple of weeks and the achievement was second only to making warrant officer.

Then it was back to the *LaSalle* where, now as CWO selectee, I decided it would be smart to learn the other divisions in supply, such as disbursing, ship's store, laundry, and the rest. Once you're selected, you're expected to start getting groomed for leading a division. But Lucas wouldn't let me go for no other reason than him just being a hater. That was fine, I thought to myself, but it was his responsibility to groom me from enlisted to officer. So I went to the Chief Engineer, Commander Tony Cardoso, and asked if I could come work for him. He said, "Sure, Chief," and got permission from the captain, and that's where I served out my time on the ship, a cook from the bridge to the engine room.

Guys like Lucas pissed me off, but by then I'd been well seasoned in dealing with his type. I felt good about myself and I knew that my service did not go unnoticed by the superiors above him. Captain Caren, in fact, thought enough of me to let me fly from Italy to DC to be a part of the commissioning of the Women in Military Service Memorial. I'd heard about this memorial and had wanted to be a part of it. You could donate as little as twenty bucks and become a charter member, which is what I did. Naturally, I wanted to be at its grand opening and dedication. The memorial commission wrote to Captain Caren requesting I be granted leave to attend, and Captain Caren readily gave it.

The ceremony was awesome. The night before there was a candlelight march from the Lincoln Memorial, across the Arlington Memorial Bridge, to the new memorial. The next morning there was a wreath-laying at the Tomb of the Unknown Soldier. Then came the dedication ceremony with over 5,000 people in Memorial Amphitheater. Bob Dole gave a speech and then the services were moved to the memorial itself where more than 30,000 had gathered. I was one of the first one-hundred women to be seated for the ceremony and was given one of the front row seats, among women who had served in both World Wars and even some who were descendants of women who had served in prior wars. I was honored. And as far as I knew, I was the only service person who had come to the ceremony from overseas duty.

There was an all-female flyover, the first in history. Then came the speeches: Vice President Al Gore, Secretary of Defense William Cohen, Justice Sandra Day O'Connor, and others. President Bill Clinton and First Lady Hillary were out of the country, but had made a taped message. Maybe the best speech was by a woman named Frieda Mae Greene Hardin. She was 101 and a veteran of World War I. She wore her World War I Navy yeoman's uniform and ended her remarks with an admonition for us women to "Go for it!" Then Kenny Rogers and Patti Austin sang a special tribute entitled, "I Will Always Remember You."

At one point during the day, I spotted Brigadier General Wilma Vaught, president of the board of directors for the foundation that raised the funds for the memorial. I introduced myself and asked if I could get a photo of the two of us. She smiled and said sure, and just before the picture was taken, she said, "Now you stand tall!"

The whole experience was magical and I'd never felt so proud of my service.

Back in Gaeta, however, I often found myself alone. Yes, as a crew, we bonded, but I was a chief and a new selectee and fraternization was frowned upon. I wasn't much of a bar or club person either. Sometimes on weekends, I'd go to Petty Officer FC2 Carl Tindall's place to jam. He'd play keyboards, SN Cedric Davis would play bass guitar, and I would sing. We'd jam the Fugee's version of *Killing Me Softly*. But outside of those occasions, I spent a lot of time by myself. Sometimes, I'd get down, but then I'd throw myself into my work. Working was always my best therapy. Or, back in the apartment, I'd pop in a cassette on positive thinking and get on my stair-stepper.

Being commissioned as Chief Warrant Officer was confirmation that I was doing things right. It meant a minimum of three more years of service, but that was fine with me. That would give me an even twenty in the Navy and I began to think that maybe retirement might be my next course of action. In my mind, my commissioning ceremony would be my retirement ceremony.

The ceremony was on the flight deck overlooking Gaeta. *Che bella giornata!* All my shipmates who had been so supportive and encouraging were present. I hand-selected each participant. Mama even came over to Italy to be there. Several shipmates made acknowledgments, including Commander Cardoso. Captain Bruce Clingan spoke, too.

While the sideboys slowly folded the flag, Commander Damon Singleton eloquently read "Old Glory": I am the flag of the United States of America. My name is Old Glory...I have fought in every battle of every war...Gettysburg, Shiloh...the trenches of France...the beaches of Normandy...I have slipped the bonds of earth...I am proud. My name is "Old Glory"—long may I wave, Dear God, long may I wave. Then I was officially commissioned as Chief Warrant Officer. I made a speech thanking everyone and I even brought Mama up on the stage. I gave her a hand-crafted Italian portrait of roses with gold writing that said, "May you always know I love you." I found tears in my eyes at several moments in the ceremony. At the end, a recording of me singing "The Way We Were" was played, a version I had made with Tindall accompanying me on piano. I dedicated it to the crew. I'd been in the Navy for seventeen years and it felt as though every hour had led to that one, my finest and proudest hour.

In the printed program for the ceremony, there was a note explaining the term traditionally given to someone who has come up through the ranks to become an officer, a person who "having hated officers all his life and now finding himself one, is a most unpleasant person to encounter when one has been late for reveille, especially since he knows all your excuses, having employed them himself in past years." The term, in a more general way, refers to "a rough person who enters polite life." It was derived from the Mexican-Spanish word mesteno, a wild horse. Translated, the term is mustang. I liked that. It fit.

All in all, I loved my time in Italy and I loved my time on the *LaSalle*. I pushed my people hard, but they did their jobs and we excelled. Years later I came across an unofficial Navy website where ships were listed with their crews over the years. You could register on the site and post comments. I posted this: "Gave my troops hell, But I loved y'all so much!"

CHAPTER 11

GOING HOME

I served on one more ship during my time in the Navy and it was the *USS Simon Lake*, a submarine tender. My time on her wasn't especially noteworthy, nothing like my time on the *LaSalle*. In fact, I had reached a point by then where I was ready to leave the Navy. I knew it even before I left the *LaSalle*.

There was no single reason, but part of my decision to retire came from my realization over time that the US Navy had become a different navy than the one I'd signed up for so many years before. I don't know, maybe the armed services were just following the trends of society, but it appeared to me that things were a lot more touchy-feely now. The toughness I remembered from my early years was now a thing of the past. Sailors were beginning to carry cell phones around and calling home all the time. I heard a story where a soldier in Afghanistan called his mother from the trenches. Female sailors began wearing their hair below the collar. Juniors and seniors were openly fraternizing. It seemed to me that the level of commitment was falling, and I wondered about the lack of discipline as compared to when I enlisted. Would we be able to carry on a war?

Also, I was finding that even as a CWO, I was being micromanaged on the *Simon Lake.* That wasn't going to work for me. I never had the freedom to do my job the way I knew it needed to be done. This was especially disappointing because it made me wonder why I'd done all the work to get to that level.

All in all, when it came right down to it, I had lost the drive and passion for the Navy that I had deeply held my entire career. I still had my Navy pride and honored the military customs and traditions, but it was time to get out. Thankfully, I'd put in twenty years and that was enough. There was no big celebration or ceremony. I'd already decided that my CWO ceremony on the *LaSalle* was my retirement party and that was all right with me.

The question, of course, became what to do with my time. I thought about some kind of counseling or mentorship position somewhere. Nada and I talked about opening a bed and breakfast. Truthfully, however, there was nothing I found myself feeling especially enthusiastic about. For twenty years, I'd been enthusiastic about the Navy. Very quickly I learned that making the adjustment from military service to civilian life was going to be difficult. I should have seen it coming. I took the Navy's TAP classes (Transitional Assistance Program), and learned all about the problems veterans have after their service, the depression and anxiety and even shortened life expectancies. And not just for PTSD veterans who have seen combat, but veterans across the board. I learned that twenty-two veterans commit suicide every day. In fact, an awareness campaign would begin in 2016 called the "22 Pushup Challenge." Participants do twenty-two pushups a day to promote awareness for veteran suicide prevention. I could understand the depression. After twenty years of knowing exactly what you're going to be doing every day, suddenly, there you are without a clue as to what to do with yourself.

At the least, I knew I needed to work. I retired in May of 2001 in Washington DC and went to work as an assistant manager at a CVS in Alexandria. That didn't last long. Employees didn't want to come to work and I found myself being micromanaged just like my last days in the Navy. I worked for Walmart after that, and then in the deli section of a Shoppers Food Warehouse. I was working at Shoppers in September of that year and one morning, on a day off, I drove to a Lowe's for some odds and ends. I got out of the car and noticed a strange smell in the air, like something was burning somewhere. Inside the store, people were talking about something that was happening, something big, but I couldn't grasp what it was they were talking about. I went back outside and saw a group of people looking off into the distance where a cloud of thick black smoke was billowing against the blue sky.

I drove straight home and turned on the TV to discover that a plane had crashed into the Pentagon. Two more planes had crashed into the World Trade Center towers in New York. Another plane was down somewhere in Pennsylvania. I lived close to the Pentagon. At that time, there was no telling how many more planes had been hijacked and where they were on their way to, but of course everyone in my area knew that Washington, DC was a prime target. We were on edge for the rest of the day, until we heard that every plane had been accounted for. Only then, that evening, did the full magnitude of the attack hit me. I had retired from military service just three months prior. Had I known what was coming, I would have stayed in. I would have continued to serve my country. How could I not have?

Not long after that, I left my job at Shoppers. I had begun having issues with both my hands. Carpal tunnel, specifically. Both hands required surgery. Plus, I was experiencing back spasms. And mentally, I needed a new start. I decided it was time to go home, time to go back to Louisville. Besides, that's where Daddy was. He was still in that nursing home, his dementia getting worse. He needed me. And I knew I needed him.

I figured I'd live with Mama and save up some money. She was happy to have me, but there was just one problem. Ricky had come home too and she'd given the upstairs bedroom to him. He'd had some ups and down, been married, been divorced, and had problems with drugs. Me, I was coming home from serving my country. But Ricky got the extra bedroom and I was relegated to the damp, musty basement. I suppose it shouldn't have been a surprise. Nevertheless, I tried to hook the place up. I repainted it, threw down some area rugs, brought in some gym equipment, and tried to make it as homey as I could.

My other brother Jerry, in the meantime, was a member of a local motorcycle club called the Flying Dragons. I'd go to the clubhouse from time to time to see Jerry and his wife Tina. One night I met a guy there named Calvin. Calvin wasn't very educated but was a streetwise brother. And a bit of a hoodlum. In fact, he was a felon fresh out of prison. But he was decent enough and he was funny. Basically, he was a fun guy to drink beer or Crown Royal with and shoot the breeze. Plus, he seemed to understand my family situation, how I was always trying to please everyone and getting nothing in return. He was the only one who seemed to get it and I guess I needed that. Some of the girls around the club tried to warn me about Calvin, but my attitude was that I was a good woman and I was sure I could turn him around. I married Calvin, more for something to do than for love. My impulsivity surprised us both.

By then, I'd been living on my own in an apartment for six months. It hadn't been easy living with Mama. I knew it would be best for our relationship if I left. I told Mama about the apartment and she said, "I hope yours is the only name on the lease." Even though Calvin always treated her with respect, she didn't like him at all. Her major concern? That Calvin was going to take all of my money. Then how would I take care of her?

I lived in the apartment alone for a while, and then Calvin moved in and we married. Whether I believed I could turn him around or not, I didn't exactly go into the marriage with a lot of commitment. I didn't even take his last name. Calvin's own brother asked me why I was marrying Calvin. It didn't take long for Calvin to start making me regret the decision. He stayed out late, began to use drugs, and accumulated a few chicks on the side. Probably the same ones who had warned me about him. Maybe more than anything, I couldn't really talk to him. We were on different levels intellectually. Half the time I felt that he couldn't relate to me and the other half of the time, I felt I couldn't relate to him. The one thing he was good for, bringing money into the house and trying to take care of me, I couldn't even appreciate because I'd become accustomed to taking care of myself. That wasn't what I was looking for in a husband. Not that I knew what I *was* looking for.

We started arguing a lot. One night I went to the club to see Jerry. Calvin was out somewhere, but who knew where? I went home knowing that Calvin would discover I'd been to the club. It was okay if he went out, but not okay if I went out. Truthfully, I rarely went out anyway. Mostly just to see Jerry and Tina at the club. Nevertheless, Calvin was always keeping tabs on me. When Calvin came home that night, I called Nada and put her on speaker so she could hear what was going to happen. Sure enough, Calvin came home furious, asking me why I was at the club. He got in my face and started talking crazy. I was in the kitchen about to prepare some fried chicken that I'd promised Jerry for a funeral repast the next day for one of his friends. It was why I'd gone to the club. Jerry gave me money for the chicken. But there was no explaining anything to Calvin. He kept grilling me on why I'd gone out.

I'd had enough. I had a frying pan full of hot oil and I said, "You want this hot grease on you now, or you wanna wait till you go to sleep?"

Calvin went into the bedroom, returning a few seconds later with a gun. He pointed it at my head and said, "You think I'm playing with you?"

I wasn't afraid. Maybe I was just too pissed off, or maybe I was just too tired of everything. "Oh, you gonna shoot me, huh?" I said.

"Yeah," he answered. "And watchoo gonna do? Call your brothers? They gonna end up in body bags too. All of ya'll are gonna end up in body bags."

"Boy, get out of my face," I said. I smudged him in the face and said, "If you gonna shoot, shoot, punk ass."

Calvin wasn't going to shoot.

I told him to get out. "Get your shit and get out now," I said.

He lowered the gun and walked back into the bedroom and commenced to packing, singing Bobby Womack's "*If you think you're lonely now, wait until tonight, girl...*" Then he left. It was well after midnight but I called maintenance and they came right over and put a new lock on the door.

After eleven months, so ended marriage number two.

Now there was nobody who understood me. Except Daddy.

I began thinking I'd made a mistake coming back to Louisville. I missed the Navy. I missed the life I had known for the previous twenty years. And Mama, well, she continued to be Mama.

I tried to keep busy by working out and baking. I made and sold rum cakes and pound cakes to supplement my income. I did some journaling, too. I had started keeping a journal years before as a way to try to make sense of things. I liked writing and it had helped. It helped now, too. It was therapeutic. The only other thing that helped was going to visit Daddy. His eyes lit up whenever I'd go see him. He'd always tell me I was pretty. I'd tell him he was handsome and he'd say, "I know." Even through the dementia, Daddy seemed to have some kind of sixth sense, telling me he loved me right when I needed to hear it the most.

I realized, however, that there weren't too many family members visiting him regularly. I was all Daddy really had and it made me cry every time I'd leave him. Plus, I didn't like the nursing home he was in. They weren't taking good care of him. He got pneumonia twice. He got urinary tract infections. Then he had a stroke. Daddy went into the hospital and it didn't seem like he was going to pull through, but he did. When he was released, I told my brothers we needed to put him in a better nursing home. They agreed.

In the meantime, I had my own problems. I had fallen into debt again. My health wasn't good and I felt depressed a lot. I started getting headaches. At one point, I had to undergo a full hysterectomy, a result of fibroids. While on the *Simon Lake*, I'd had fibroid surgery, but the fibroids had come back. Nevertheless, during this period, I decided to add to the associate degree I had earned in the Navy, enrolling in an accelerated, eighteen-month program at Indiana Wesleyan to earn a BS in business management.

Afterward, I began volunteering at my cousin's food ministry, which I found rewarding. I traveled a lot, too. I'd get in my truck and ride. Long drives were therapeutic. But my depression was getting worse. There were all of the obvious reasons—my health issues, leaving the Navy, Mama's constant downpour of negativity, seeing Daddy in such a fragile state—but my depression was there regardless. In truth, I had been receiving counseling since before my retirement. I'd been depressed and serving on the *Simon Lake* had exacerbated my depression. I frequently found myself tearful, with feelings of hopelessness and being out of control. I didn't sleep well. Dr. Luis Fernandez, a clinical psychologist, recommended limited duty. For underlying causes to my depression, he noted work stress and a personality style of "hard-working perfectionism." I hadn't really thought of it before, but it was true. I was a perfectionist and it was a grueling way to approach life.

But now, with retirement, I was feeling even more depressed and hopeless. I never felt suicidal, but I often felt as if I had nothing more to offer. Maybe there was nothing left for me.

I went to the VA for continued counseling. Then, finally, came the tests. The psychological assessments. First in 2004, and then again in 2006. And the resulting diagnosis, after forty-five years of life, helped explain everything.

CHAPTER 12

ADHD

Once I received the diagnosis, I began to think back over my life, and a whole bunch of things that seemed random at the time—emotions, behaviors, my mental functioning—started making sense and seemed not so random after all, especially after I started learning more about ADHD.

The major outward symptoms of adult attention deficit/hyperactivity disorder are well known and pretty well described by the name of the disorder itself: difficulty paying attention and restless hyperactivity. But these symptoms can accompany, or lead to, other symptoms, some more subtle than others. A person living with ADHD can have a low tolerance for frustration. They can have a quick temper. Often they have trouble coping with stress. They might be impulsive, even reckless. They may be disorganized or have problems with time management. They can have mood swings.

They can suffer from depression and anxiety.

The term ADHD came about in 1987, but the disorder was recognized by physicians as early as the mid-1700s. There were people who exhibited the standard behaviors and with no explainable cause. The condition was noticed mostly in children, but it was recognized in adults as well. It wasn't studied very seriously until the twentieth century, however, when it went by names like "minimal brain dysfunction," "learning" or "behavior disability," or simply "hyperactivity." The 1968 *Diagnostic and Statistical Manual of Mental Disorders*, kind of the bible of the American Psychiatric Association, called it "Hyperkinetic Reaction of Childhood." But of course hyperactivity is just one symptom, and it's not always present. Eventually the term ADD, for "Attention Deficit Disorder" came into use, followed by today's attention deficit/hyperactivity disorder, which has the advantage of highlighting both major symptoms. Often, as in my case, the word "Adult" precedes the initials to differentiate it from a childhood disorder.

But it starts in childhood. Estimates vary, but it's generally believed that about five percent of children have it. Thirty to fifty percent of them will continue to have symptoms into adulthood. For some, the symptoms may lessen. Others may not be so fortunate and that's the camp I fall into.

Nobody knows the exact cause, but there does seem to be a genetic component. Environmental factors might play a part, like if you were exposed to lead from pipes and paint in older buildings. It's also believed a person's risk increases if their birth mother smoked or drank during pregnancy. For the record, my mother did both.

Learning all of this was eye-opening. And, strangely, something of a relief. I thought back to all the difficulties I had in school. Everyone else seemed so much smarter than me. I couldn't focus like they could. I was frustrated. The teachers were frustrated. I even almost flunked home economics! But now I knew why. I wasn't stupid. I wasn't slow. I simply didn't have the tools that everyone else had. I didn't have the patience and the ability to concentrate. It was never a matter of intelligence and it was never a lack of desire to succeed.

The diagnosis also explained the lifelong depression and anxiety. I say lifelong, because I distinctly remember that time when Miss Bishop, my fifth grade teacher, commented on my report card that I was "feeling bad." My sixth grade teacher, Miss McShan, said that I lacked confidence, and it's no wonder.

Depression is known as a "comorbid" or coexisting condition with ADHD. Depression in this case refers to the clinical use of the term, not just the routine down-in-the-dumps feeling you might have on a rainy day. We're talking about depression that might go on for weeks, a kind of general overall feeling of sadness, often accompanied by anxiety. Half the people who have ADHD end up seeking help for depression. Just like me.

I sought help for something else, too: the feeling I could never shake that something was wrong with me. This was not just depression. This was a feeling of isolation. I knew only that something was either wrong with me or something was wrong with everybody else. Either way, I was alone and alienated. I didn't fit in anywhere.

Naturally, this only made the underlying depression worse, which, when you added it all up, led to that initial psychological assessment of dysthymic depression, otherwise known as persistent depressive disorder. It's hard to diagnose ADHD sometimes because the symptoms are so similar to depression. Depression causes one to lose focus, to lose patience, to be more prone to anger, to be reckless, to have trouble coping with stress. In other words, ADHD can look a lot like depression. It was only with the second assessment, with more comprehensive testing, that the true source of my depression was revealed.

Being a coexisting condition means that the depression isn't necessarily caused by the ADHD, although having ADHD with all its accompanying symptoms, sure is depressing enough. But sometimes the depression is just there, just hanging out, even when things are going well for me. There doesn't seem to be a reason for it and that's the way it is with a lot of people with ADHD. The link between depression and ADHD is another one of those things that isn't really understood very well.

This idea of being depressed or anxious or stressed-out for no real reason was a constant theme of my Navy career. In the writing of this book, to better remember the events of my life, I looked back over my record and was stunned by what I had accomplished. I honestly had no idea. To me, living those days, it seemed as if I could never get my shit together. Just like in school, everybody else seemed focused but me. Everyone else was organized. I felt as if I had to work twice as hard. Time after time in my journal, I wrote that I was feeling "unproductive."

In fact, I did work twice as hard. After all, working hard is what kept me going and kept me focused. In military parlance, I was a "hard charger." And that was my therapy. The discipline of the Navy, from boot camp onward, forced me to stay on track. The work required organization and structure. These are like gold nuggets to a person with ADHD. At Point Mugu, they called me "recipe card cook" because of my obsessiveness with the recipe card instructions.

Once I learned I had been living with ADHD, that obsessiveness made perfect sense. To this day, I use my recipe cards, even when I'm baking a cake I might have baked a hundred times. To this day, I also still journal that I often feel unproductive, even when all the evidence says otherwise.

My hyperactivity made perfect sense, too. I remembered those times when Jay would make me stop and slow down. I was going ten different directions at once. But now I knew that this was normal for someone with ADHD. I was not crazy, after all.

In fact, as I learned more about it, I began to understand that maybe attention deficit/hyperactivity disorder is not so much a disorder after all. Dr. Edward Hallowell, a psychiatrist and *New York Times* bestselling author, and Dr. John Ratey, an associate clinical professor of psychiatry at Harvard Medical School, have both written extensively on ADHD, coauthoring several books about the subject including *Driven to Distraction* and *ADHD 2.0: New Science and Essential Strategies for Thriving with Distraction—from Childhood Through Adulthood*. They both seem to think ADHD needs a new name and have suggested VAST: variable attention stimulus trait.

First off, this name omits the word "disorder." Hallowell and Ratey don't like the idea that the condition is thought of as a disease. In their estimation, it's not a disease. It's a personality trait. Secondly, "variable attention stimulus" recognizes that the condition doesn't equate to a *lack* of attention. Far from it. I can attest that it's much more like too much attention. Too many things coming at you at once, stopping you completely in your tracks while you try to figure out which thing to focus on. You pay attention to *everything*. It's like facing a firehose every day. As Hallowell puts it, it's having a Ferrari brain with bicycle brakes. The end result is often disorganization and problems with time management. Sometimes, when someone is talking to me, it's overwhelming because I'm trying to grasp every word and I end up losing the context. Then the words just sort of morph into something meaningless, as though I'm being spoken to by Charlie Brown's teacher. Of course, I'll nod along, as if I'm following everything being said to me.

I also learned more about that accompanying depression I'd experienced. Well-known ADHD clinician Dr. William Dodson has written of *rejection sensitive dysphoria*, a very specific type of depression experienced only by people living with ADHD. Essentially, it's depression mixed with huge amounts of shame and guilt. People like me are way more sensitive to rejection and criticism. We live in fear of disappointing important people in our lives. The problem is that the ADHD brain has a hard time sorting out emotions. Everyone feels guilt and shame at times, but most people's brains properly regulate it. People without ADHD—or without similar neuro conditions, like autism or dyslexia, for example, people that the scientific community has taken to referencing as "neurotypical" people—can put their guilt and shame within a proper, healthy context. Not so with a person living with ADHD. Naturally, this leads to depression, frustration, hopelessness, and, in the case of some folks with ADHD (like me) outbursts of anger.

I've felt them all. It is any wonder I've had to deal with my temper all my life? Is it any wonder my mother's remarks and criticisms stung so harshly? Of course it didn't help that my mother knew they stung and used that knowledge in manipulative ways.

One encouraging thing I learned was that there are a lot of smart people out there who have dedicated themselves to the study of ADHD. Besides Hallowell, Ratey, and Dodd, I became acquainted with the work of Dr. Russell Barkley. Dr. Barkley has written a bunch of books and scientific papers about AHDH and also made some YouTube videos. He calls ADHD the diabetes of psychiatry, a chronic disorder that requires daily management to prevent the secondary harms it can cause. In one of those YouTube videos, he explains something very fundamental about the condition. With people who are living with ADHD, there is a distinct split between the rear part of the brain, which is in charge of knowledge, and the front part of the brain, which is in charge of performance.

As Dr. Barkley puts it: "You can know stuff, but you won't do stuff." It's a disorder, that is to say, of *intention*, not *attention*. When I heard this, it resonated so completely that I almost fell out of my chair. I have no lack of knowledge. I *know* to do something. But getting myself to execute it is another thing altogether.

My education in ADHD explained so much. It didn't cure it, of course. There is no cure. But it gave me something almost as valuable: self-awareness. I might not be able to help slipping into depression or anger, and I might not be able to control my focus or execute, but at least I now knew *why*.

These were powerful revelations. And they allowed me to stand back and look at what was happening to me in a more objective way. I might be depressed for no apparent reason one day, but rather than wallow in the depression and allow it to possibly morph into anxiety, I can say, "Shay, that's just the ADHD." I go into my self-awareness zone and recapture enough positive energy to counteract the anxiety.

And there was something else positive that I learned. According to Ratey and Hallowell, other characteristics of ADHD include toughness and a propensity to never give up. I can attest to that, too. Again, this was not something I knew about myself until I went back and looked at the record, the unbiased documentation of my Navy career. But it's all there. Maybe it's because we ADHD people have to work harder. Maybe it's because nothing comes easy to us. We have to be hard-charging. But over time, we find ways to move forward. Our hurdles become steppingstones. We become better not in spite of our obstacles, but because of them. We learn to accept the challenges. We learn toughness. And we never give up. Ever.

CHAPTER 13

NO RESPECT

Okay, so if we know now what ADHD is, what can be done about it? Yes, there's no cure, but are there treatment options and ways to combat the condition on a day-to-day basis? After all, ADHD is more prevalent than most people think. Here's a random sampling of people you may have heard of who are living with ADHD: Bill Gates, Justin Timberlake, Terry Bradshaw, Trevor Noah, James Carville, Michael Phelps, Ryan Gosling, Adam Levine, Ty Pennington, Simone Biles, Howie Mandel, Michael Jordan, Whoopi Goldberg. I could probably list a hundred more without having to search very hard for names.

You'd think, then, with all these examples, that it must be a pretty easy condition to diagnose. Well, we know it's sometimes difficult because of its similarities to clinical depression. But there's another reason it's often missed, an inexcusable reason: doctors don't look for it.

Too many doctors are too quick to prescribe medications for various conditions without really bothering to find the source of the symptoms. Depressed? Here, take some anti-depressants. But what if, before jumping to conclusions, doctors were trained to ask a few basic questions first. Questions like, "Do you frequently have trouble concentrating?" "Do you often find yourself feeling fidgety?" "Do you find it hard to plan ahead or prioritize?" "Do you act impulsively?" "Do you recall always being like this?"

Simple questions. But extraordinarily significant. The doctor doesn't have to be an expert in ADHD. All he or she has to do is determine whether or not there's a likelihood of ADHD. A simple questionnaire would allow the doctor to do just this. Then, the doctor can refer the patient to someone who can make a more definitive diagnosis. I really do believe it's just that simple.

As I noted, just receiving the diagnosis was huge for me. Knowing I wasn't crazy, lazy, or stupid was liberating.

The proper diagnosis is a big first step. Unfortunately, just like with me, it often gets missed. Dr. Russell Barkley, the doctor who talks about the split between the part of the brain in charge of knowledge and the part of the brain in charge of performance, calls ADHD the Rodney Dangerfield of disorders. It gets no respect.

It's even worse for people of color. Multiple studies have shown that Black children are 70 percent less likely to receive an ADHD diagnosis than White children. And it's worse still for Black females. René Brooks, a Black woman with ADHD has written extensively about her experiences and about the unique problems Black women have, not just in getting diagnosed and treated for ADHD, but within the medical community as a whole. Black women in general aren't taken as seriously, and the problem is exacerbated by the role that Black women have within their *own* community. As Brooks points out, we're supposed to be quiet and strong and in control of our emotions. We're supposed to conform. We're supposed to rely on our faith for comfort and treatment. So the problem is two-fold: we don't seek help, and when we do, our problems are often more quickly dismissed than those of our white counterparts.

But ADHD is not taken as seriously as other mental conditions regardless of a patient's gender or color. I want to believe that will all change as medical science continues to make progress and awareness grows.

Assuming a proper diagnosis, what next? I've talked about self-awareness. Being able to know why you're struggling with something, or being able to understand why you might be feeling depressed and anxious, is half the battle. For some people this might mean actually admitting to the problem. We live in a society that teaches us not to show, or admit to, something that might be perceived as a "weakness." We need to be strong. We need to have faith. I tried to explain to my cousin Beverly one time the difficulties I was having with my very real, *clinical* condition. Her response was, "Cuz, you can't claim all that mess. Just give it to God." I said, "Cuz, I did give it to God and he told me to get help!" ADHD exists. I accomplish things, but it might take days where it takes a neurotypical person hours. It's impossible to not "claim" this. And it would be unhealthy and counterproductive. I struggle and I need help and that's just the way it is.

Some people I just don't share it with at all. Some folk think a good cup of coffee will level you out. Over the years, I've learned not to tell everyone. Either I don't explain it easily enough for them, or they don't receive it easily enough.

If awareness/admittance is half the battle, what's the other half? First, medication is entirely appropriate. To this day, I take methylphenidate, a central nervous system stimulant. It works on chemicals and nerves in the brain to counteract hyperactivity and impulse control, allowing the brain to better focus. Interestingly, I took this drug (by the brand name Concerta) even before my ADHD diagnosis. I'd taken it while attending college. The doctor had told me it was often given to kids to help them focus in school. Lack of focus was part of the depression I was originally diagnosed with.

In addition to medication, there are things Dr. Barkley recommends that can help someone living with ADHD to improve their performance, even with the split between the back of the brain and the front. I can confirm that these strategies work because I use them myself, at least when I'm in my disciplined mode and in my routine. First off, you have to take mental information and make it physical. Take it out of the brain, in other words. What does this mean? It means using to-do lists and writing out reminders on post-it notes. When I write something on a post-it note, I can see it. I don't have to think through it. I bridge that split. And believe me, I have post-it notes everywhere.

The same principle applies with time management and deadlines. You can tell me that I need to finish something by next Tuesday, but that information is going to sit inside my brain and get hung up somewhere between knowledge and performance. This makes me an active procrastinator. Again, I need to take the deadline out of my head. Depending on the task, you can use a timer, a clock, a calendar, or reminders from a smart phone. It's best, too, if you break the task down into component parts, each due by a specific time or day and, again, noted by something *external* to the brain. (This is something I'm still working on.)

Dr. Barkley is also a proponent of cognitive behavioral therapy for people with ADHD. CBT is a sort of talk therapy where you face your negative thinking, combating it with reason and rational thought. It's an extension of the awareness idea, where you realize it's not helpful to blame yourself for an inherent brain condition. Dr. J. Russell Ramsay, author, along with Dr. Anthony Rostain, of *Cognitive Behavioral Therapy for Adult ADHD* talks about the negative things we say to ourselves, and I sure as hell know the negative things I've said to *myself* over the years. It's commonplace for people with ADHD but, as Ramsey points out, it can be managed with the right therapist who's skilled not only in CBT, but also in ADHD.

Doctors Steven Safren, Susan Sprich, Carol Perlman, and Michael Otto have put together a whole CBT program for ADHD, complete with a workbook: *Mastering Your Adult ADHD: A Cognitive Behavioral Treatment Program*. And Dr. Mary Solanto's book *Cognitive Behavioral Therapy for Adult ADHD: Targeting Executive Dysfunction* is another great resource.

CBT can help with making sense of emotions, too. Part of the mood swings and anxiety comes from the way in which ADHD prevents a normal response to events that bring anger or frustration. Most people can properly regulate the feelings of disappointment, for instance. They can take actions that make themselves feel better, or reason with themselves that maybe things aren't so bad. They get over the negative feelings, sometimes sooner, sometimes later. A person with ADHD, on the other hand, has trouble regulating. Their brain gets flooded with emotions. As I've noted, they feel anger and frustration intensely. It's too much to handle. This is why we lose our tempers and lash out or take impulsive, sometimes harmful, actions. CBT works to talk us down from the ledge.

It's scary when I think of the times I could have done something harmful because of my executive functioning disorder. Thankfully, the Navy provided me with the discipline and structure necessary to prevent me from doing anything too crazy.

And that's a strategy, too: structure. ADHD/Executive Function consultant, coach, and speaker Brendan Mahan talks about structure as a critical part of a healthy ADHD lifestyle. He also encourages good sleeping habits and a proper diet. Mahan has a podcast called "ADHD Essentials" where he discusses the day-to-day things a person living with ADHD can do to make their lives better. An example that struck close to home with me: getting a better handle on the misperceptions we have of ourselves. Mahan talks about how he still bases his self-worth on how he did in middle school! No matter what I did in the Navy, it seems I could not escape the feelings I'd brought with me from childhood. I wasn't smart. I couldn't succeed. I couldn't be productive. Everything was hard for me when it was so easy for everyone else. And yet throughout my career, all the evidence said otherwise. I was extraordinarily productive. I just couldn't get myself to believe it.

One particular type of behavioral therapy that I'm particularly familiar with is ACT: Acceptance and Commitment Therapy. ACT teaches you to embrace your feelings and thoughts, rather than to try to ignore them or feel guilty because of them. It's linked with mindfulness, allowing you to grasp objectively what you're feeling in the moment, being an *observer*. I've explored ACT with my VA group and I've also taken advantage of the many YouTube videos on the subject, especially by some of the foremost experts in the field, guys like Steven Hayes and Russ Harris.

Of course, I'd done therapy going back to Chaplain Judy Cadenhead at Anacostia. Mostly it had been talk therapy and there had been a few therapists along the way, up to and including Dr. Luis Fernandez whom I saw while assigned to the *Simon Lake*, the psychologist who recommended limited duty. After Fernandez, by the way, came Dr. Brian Goodwin. I'll always remember Dr. Goodwin for a certain word he used to describe me, one I'd never really taken note of before: *resilient*. I looked it up and decided that I liked that word. Yep, that's me. But with my diagnosis, my approach to therapy became more appropriate for my condition, like with ACT. I also engage in yoga, meditation, Tai chi, and exercise, all of which are designed to bring me into the *now*, to shut off that firehose of thoughts. After all, when you stop and think about it, there is *only* now.

In the end, however, for people living with ADHD, all the workarounds and medications and therapies are useless without a proper diagnosis. On a societal level, that's the key to the management of ADHD. There has to be more awareness, both inside and outside the medical profession. After all, it's much more common than people think, worthy of a lot more respect than what it gets. There are people out there who need help. People who don't even know they have ADHD. People who are trying to make sense of their cognitive difficulties and their mood swings and depression. People who are anxious and who feel isolated. People who are hurting. They don't know what to do because they don't understand what's wrong with them. The difference between being diagnosed and being undiagnosed is the difference between day and night. Too many people are living in darkness. I'd like to see more effort being put into identifying these people so that, as a society, we can begin to help them.

CHAPTER 14

GET IT IN WRITING

One therapeutic workaround for ADHD deserves its own chapter. I first discovered the value of journaling in tenth grade, although I had no idea that's what it was called. It was a routine English assignment. An essay. We could write about whatever we wanted to and I wrote about how my mother didn't trust me. I felt better immediately. As I was writing, it was as if I had someone to talk to. And there was something magical about the act of putting words together, the creation of sentences and paragraphs, making tangible the thoughts that had been bouncing around my head. It felt like such an accomplishment. And it didn't hurt that the teacher gave me an A-plus.

I was further encouraged at the University of Louisville. An English professor told me to keep up my writing. I've been journaling steadily ever since. I have few rules about it. When the mood strikes—when I feel the need to work something out in words—I sit down with a pen and a notebook and I let the words pour out onto the page. I've journaled pretty much everywhere, even in church. My preferences are outdoor patios, coffee shops, or in the booths of casual restaurants.

That said, I do try to make an effort to journal something every morning. Julia Cameron in *Morning Pages Journal*, the companion book to her classic *The Artist's Way*, encourages the writer to write three pages first thing in the morning, clearing away the distractions of the prior day. Cameron calls journaling "spiritual windshield wipers." And morning is a great time because it's before the daily obstacles come along that can impede one's creativity. And what does one write? Anything. Just write. Get it all off your chest, the good and the bad. From the noise of your neighbor's kids to how beautiful the sun is shining. Stream-of-consciousness is a great way to start. Before you know it, you're focused on a topic or theme that is, suddenly, uppermost in your mind. Sometimes I'm surprised by what I end up writing about. It might be nothing like what I start out with. Sometimes it's difficult to get started. But then I get into a groove and before I know it, I've filled way more than Cameron's three pages. Things just start flowing from my mind to my pen to the paper. I've noticed different handwritings from one day to the next. Looking back at older writings, I can tell by the style whether I was anxious, sad, angry, or calm.

I try to journal every day, but there are times when I don't. I've made it a high priority but sometimes life gets in the way. Sometimes it's a struggle and I simply can't bring myself to open a notebook. I used to give myself a hard time about these missed days, but am much more lenient with myself now. I might miss a day, but I know that sooner or later, I will jump back on it. I cannot imagine not journaling for any real length of time, even though in my Navy career, there were periods of journal inactivity that lasted months. But always, I came back to it.

Most of the time I write to myself, and sometimes even in dialogue. There have been times in my life when there simply wasn't anyone else to talk to. Through journaling, I found myself becoming my biggest cheerleader. "Shay, you gotta keep pluggin'," I'd write, and often still do.

When Daddy was in his worst health, I'd journal to him. "Daddy, I love you and think about you so much." I've journaled to him since his passing, telling him how much I've missed him.

I journaled to my mother, as well, writing the things I wanted to say to her. "You prey on my miseries," I wrote one time. "It's enough that you're not the kind of mother that I can go to to share my deepest thoughts and my problems. Why do you always have to share with everybody else what Sharon's doing wrong? Why?"

Sometimes I write to God. I didn't realize this when I started. I was just writing and then one day it occurred to me that it was God who was the intended audience. I write of my gratitude, even on days when things might not be going well. I might write three pages of lament, but then I'll make a point of letting Him know how thankful I am for all that He's done for me and all that I have. It sets the perfect tone as I begin my day. And I like the idea of sometimes giving God a shout without having to get on my knees in some kind of formal, prim, solemn prayer. I just talk to Him.

Author and podcaster Ryan Holiday says to forget any "rules" about journaling. Do what works for you. He recommends just getting started, even if it's one line a day. Holiday is a Stoic, a believer in the philosophy of approaching life pragmatically, with reason, and without complaint. He quotes freely from the likes of Epictetus, Seneca, and Marcus Aurelius—famous Stoics. Stoicism is taking what comes and being indifferent to pain or pleasure. For Holiday, journalism is a way to get there and stay there. He advises leaving all of your destructive and negative thoughts in your journal.

That last piece of wisdom helps particularly with my ADHD. This is why journaling is such a valuable tool for me. When I get down on myself, when I get overwhelmed, when I get depressed, journaling helps me get the negativity out of my system. It also helps me focus, an extraordinarily beneficial advantage for someone who has trouble focusing. When you're journaling, you're in the present and you're typically writing about one thing, the most critical thing on your mind. And so journaling becomes a way to prioritize.

There's another general benefit. Journaling is a way to accurately record the events of your life. You can go back through and revisit your past, discover how you really felt at the time about something or someone, and recollect the details. Sometimes, you'll come across something farsighted, almost prophetic. On a page from a journal long ago, I found this: *One of these days, maybe I'll take all these notes and write a book.* Now how prophetic was that?

Chapter 15

The Man in My Life

Around the time I had gotten Daddy into a better nursing home, I also took guardianship. Jerry seemed relieved. He'd been guardian out of obligation. I took guardianship out of love.

As Daddy's health deteriorated, I spent more and more time with him. I'd visit with him during the days and sometimes I'd go in the middle of the night to check on him. There had been cases of residents falling out of their beds. Sure enough, on a few occasions I came in to see that they had failed to put up one of Daddy's bedrails. I had to monitor his incontinent care, too. It was a better nursing home than the previous one but it still had its problems. I placed a dry erase board in his room with a checklist of the CNA's daily duties. I was forever having to ask questions about Daddy's overall care. They'd tell me he was doing good whenever I called for a wellness check, but then I'd surprise them by doing a drive-by only to find out I wasn't getting the truth. It was a constant battle with the staff and the once-a-week doctor.

I'd bring Daddy food sometimes because they were never consistent in serving the residents their meals on time. Daddy loved chitlins. Even though I despised the smell and taste of them, I'd clean and prepare chitlins for him on holidays. Other times, I'd bring him fried green tomatoes, KFC occasionally, and sometimes White Castle burgers. Mainly, I brought sweets. I'd make him a chess pie—a southern, custard-like dessert made of eggs, butter, and sugar. He loved chess pie. I'd stop at Starbucks on the way and buy him a strawberry frappuccino. Daddy loved Tootsie Roll lollipops and my main daughterly role was to keep that lollipop jar filled.

I noticed the CNAs didn't spend a lot of time on Daddy's personal grooming at the nursing home, at least to where his grooming was up to my standards, so I'd keep his head cleanshaven, wash his feet and trim his toenails, and moisturize his dry skin. I'd plug in his favorite DVDs and give him a total spa treatment. Tootsie Roll pop in his mouth, he'd watch Sinbad, *Sanford and Son*, and the Three Stooges, all of which he'd seen a hundred times yet he'd crack up with laughter like he'd never seen them before.

Often, out of the blue, he'd turn to me and say, "I love you, baby." Once, I said to him, "Daddy, who's going to take care of me when *I* get old?" He smiled and said, "I will," and somehow in that moment, it seemed possible.

As often as I could, I'd take Daddy out of the nursing home. Sometimes, I'd take him to Vermont Liquors where he could holler at his buddies. Frequently, I'd take him to my place. Once again, Mama would say, "Sharon, you gotta be careful with that. They gonna take JW's Medicaid away." Whether she actually believed that or not, I can't say. But it was consistent with her M.O. to drive a wedge between Daddy and me. Looking back, it seems likely that that was the main reason behind the comments. After the stroke, Daddy had trouble feeding himself and on one of the infrequent times Mama came to visit, I was helping him eat. "J.W., you mean you can't feed yourself?!" Mama said. All I could say was, "*Dang*, Ma."

By then, my relationships with my brothers were strained. With nine years between us, Jerry and I had never really been close. Ricky and I were closer when growing up, but our relationship wasn't one of any real depth. That just wasn't the way Ricky was. He was a recovering alcoholic and I heard from him often, but it was mainly when he needed something from me. I didn't hear from Jerry as much. It was always me reaching out to him, but I was cool with that. Jerry was always a reserved fellow. As our parents got older and needed more help from us, I noticed I was the only one pitching in. Hearing aids, car repairs, clothes, things around the house—I'd ask about us all going in together to buy what was needed, but when it came down to it, I rarely got any financial support. I didn't get any emotional support either, which I finally determined neither brother was capable of. There had been so many times I'd helped both Ricky and Jerry, always trying to be the good, loving sister. Always giving; never getting anything in return.

Of course, Mama didn't much notice the help I'd give her. It didn't matter what I did, it was never enough. Daddy on the other hand appreciated everything I did. His health, meanwhile, was continuing to slide downhill. He kept getting infections. His foot became infected so badly that it became gangrenous and in 2014, his leg was amputated at the knee. He was in and out of the hospital with pneumonia. By January of 2015, he needed a catheter. And then, on a cold February morning in 2015, Daddy made one last trip to the hospital. He had sepsis. His body was shutting down.

Not long after I arrived at the ER, they moved Daddy to a separate room. Shortly after that, a doctor came into the room and reported to me that Daddy had sepsis, the body's radical response to infection that quickly leads to tissue damage and organ failure. There was no reversing it. The doctor asked me if Daddy had a Do Not Resuscitate order. I said yes. It was a no-brainer that Daddy was about to leave me. Then the doctor told me it would be best to move Daddy upstairs to a hospice room.

It was about ten in the morning. I called Jerry and texted Ricky. As for Mama, I decided not to call her. Jerry came but it was while Daddy was being transported to the hospice room. He didn't stick around. Ricky never came at all. I called a couple of cousins later on, after Daddy had gotten settled into the hospice room. Stephanie came right away to say goodbye to Daddy and to see how I was doing. Later that night, my cousin Larry, a minister, called and he had me put the phone to Daddy's ear and he prayed for him, for which I will always be grateful.

Soon after that, at 11:25 pm, Daddy passed away. It was just me and Daddy in the room, alone together for the last time. Before he went, I told him again how much I loved him. I held his face in my hands and said, "I love you, Daddy. Thank you for loving me." He heard me. His breathing was shallow, but I felt him doing his best to tell me that he loved me back. And then he was gone and I said a prayer, thanking God for the life of John Wesley Rucker. I lay beside him for a little while, just like I used to at the nursing home.

For the funeral, I toyed with the idea of putting Daddy in a University of Kentucky sweatsuit because he'd been such a Wildcat fan his whole life. In the end, he was dressed in his best suit, but at least the casket was UK blue, and with the wildcat logo on the top interior panel. Reverend Perryman of Perryman's Mortuary saw to that. Daddy was holding a Tootsie Roll pop, too.

Jerry and Ricky met me at the mortuary for the arrangements. I'd entered a pre-burial contract with Reverend Perryman years before and had been paying all along for both Mama and Daddy's funerals. Now, as the arrangements were being finalized for Daddy's, I had Reverend Perryman ask everyone about the balance, even though I'd paid it. I wanted to give Jerry and Ricky one more shot to help me with the expenses, and maybe for us all to come together. Wishful thinking. "Looks like we just have a balance of $900," Reverend Perryman said. "How do you want to pay for that?" Jerry and Ricky hemmed and hawed. Ricky, all six-feet-four, 230 pounds of him, basically became invisible. Finally, I said, "Listen, I'll take care of it. Ya'll pay me if ya'll ever feel like it."

For the service in the chapel, four chairs were set up in front of the casket, one for me, one for Mama, one for Ricky, and one for Jerry. I was the only one sitting there. Mama and Ricky were to the side and Jerry was somewhere in the back. My friend Kim eventually came up and sat with me so that I didn't have to sit through my father's funeral alone.

Larry presided over the service at my request and spoke eloquently, mentioning all of Daddy's children and saying that God was watching over us. A couple of Daddy's buddies from Vermont Liquors spoke a few words. Then Ricky had to make his presence known. He stood in front of everyone in his fur coat to inform us all that he had taken Daddy to his Hill Street Baptist Church and personally seen to it that he'd been saved. Good old Ricky. Meanwhile, I knew that the minister of Ricky's church hadn't even made himself available for Daddy's funeral. That's why I'd called Larry. My anger issues were starting to flame up but somehow I managed to remain calm.

My cousin Denise, Larry's wife, sang "Changed" and toward the end of the song, she pulled me up front to sing with her. I hadn't planned to, but there I was singing, *A change, a change has come over me; He changed my life and now I'm free.* I looked around at my family members and realized how true the lyrics were. How changed I was from when I was young; how changed I was from these people. How different. I wasn't part of them anymore and it felt like freedom.

And then I spoke. Just like taking care of Daddy while he was alive, I knew everyone was there out of family obligation. The whole chapel reeked of superficiality. I said, "I know everyone's got an opinion of my dad, but I thought I'd share a side of him that I don't think anybody here knows about. This is what he wrote to me once in a letter. This is who he really was and what he meant to me." And then I read a poem he'd written to me:

I am always here to understand you.
I am always here to laugh with you.
I am always here to cry with you.
I am always here to talk to you.
I am always here to think with you.
I am always here to plan with you.
Even though we might not always be together,
please know that I'm always here to love you,
—Daddy

The chapel became solemn, but if anyone was moved by the poem, or surprised by it, I didn't see it. But I knew it must have taken them all aback. They didn't know my Daddy like I'd known my Daddy.

There was a short service at the gravesite and then I went home where Nada was waiting for me. She had come for support. Then Mama called to tell me about all the things Reverend Perryman should have done differently for the service. Looking back, she was probably just upset about the letter I'd read. She hadn't known about it and I'm sure it must have made her jealous. I said, "Mama, are you serious? They just put Daddy in the ground," and I hung up the phone.

In the days and weeks that followed, I journaled to Daddy a lot. I wrote about how it seemed strange to be out driving somewhere but not taking the same roads that, for such a long time, had taken me to visit him in the nursing home. I told him how much I wanted to go back there with a chess pie for him. I told him I was sorry that I couldn't have done more for him in his last days. I told him how I cried, just a little bit, at his gravesite. I told him I felt empty. But I told him that, for his sake, I was going to keep plugging. I knew that's what he'd want me to do. And I told him that his passing was making me feel closer to Jesus. In a sense, maybe Daddy had been right. Maybe he was taking care of me like he said he would.

I also told him I was more or less done with the Rucker family. I needed to move on. Two months after the funeral, Jerry came over with a $200 contribution for his part of the funeral costs. I'm still waiting on something from Ricky.

CHAPTER 16

THE MOST LOYAL

Sometime before Daddy died, I'd started having headaches. Twice my doctor sent me to an optometrist, believing the problem to be with my eyes. Both times, I received new prescriptions for glasses. Neither prescription helped and I decided that maybe I was just going to have to live with chronic headaches, putting the condition down to the stresses of taking care of Daddy, especially when I wasn't getting much help from the rest of the Ruckers.

But things got worse, even after Daddy had passed. My vision was becoming blurred. Then I started having problems with my speech. It sounded to me as if I were stuttering, as if there were a delay in my words.

One day, while driving to Kim's in the west end of town to drop off a pie I'd made for her, Ricky called. He was at Mama's that day and he wanted me to stop by. I knew, like always, that there was something he probably needed from me and I braced myself to tell him that I didn't have any money to give him. It was bad enough that he'd asked me to come to Mama's. I dreaded going there. I was almost to Kim's when he called again asking where I was and what was taking so long. Then he hung up on me. My stress-o-meter was already blown. This sent me over the edge. I made a U-turn and went directly to Mama's. I stormed into her house. She was at the kitchen table reading the paper like nothing was wrong. Ricky was in the bathroom sitting on the toilet reading the newspaper. I burst in and said, "What the hell you hang up on me for?!"

"Man, get out of here!" he said.

I lost it. All the stress I'd felt myself under for the previous six months came pouring out of me. It's probably a good thing I don't remember everything I screamed to both Ricky and Mama, but I do recall Mama saying, "Sharon, you're going to have a stroke."

"What would ya'll care if I did?" I yelled back, and then I marched out of the house, slamming the door behind me.

Kim never did get her pie. Afterward, I drove to the Y for my Forever Fit class. I was doing light aerobics and suddenly it felt like my eyes were burning. Behind my eyes it felt as if I were being stabbed by a thousand needles. I made it to the floor and someone asked me if I was all right. Then someone else brought me water while the medical person on staff checked me out and quickly dialed 911. EMS showed up and I told them I was sure I'd be okay.

"Well, if you can get up and move around," one of them said. "we'll be on our way."

Sounded easy enough. But then I tried to stand and it felt as if miniature bombs were exploding in my head, pushing me right back down to the floor. The next thing I know, they were carrying me out of the Y on a stretcher. The burning sensation was excruciating. The lighting inside the gym was blinding and outside it was so painful that I had to slide my headband down over my eyes.

I asked the EMS guys to take me to the VA hospital where the doctors did an angiogram and discovered a ruptured blood vessel in my brain, a subarachnoid hemorrhage, I was told.

"We've got a problem, Miss Jordan," the doctor explained to me. "We can't determine where the bleed is coming from. I'm going to have you transported to the University of Louisville Hospital."

And then I overhead him talking to the EMS driver. "I don't know what shortcuts you know," he said, "but you need to get her there *fast*."

On the throbbing, bumpy ride in the ambulance, I was in too much pain to think very much about the instruction the doctor gave to the driver, but I did have the thought that I might be soon checking out.

I made a silent prayer to God. Told Him I was pretty tired anyway. I'd given it everything I had. Somehow, massive headache and all, I found peace in that drive.

At the U of L Hospital, they did another angiogram, but with no better luck finding the source of the leak than they'd had at the VA. Then they brought the chief neurologist in and he did his own angiogram, finding the source of the hemorrhage and stemming the bleeding using endovascular coiling. In such a procedure, platinum coils are passed through a catheter inserted through an artery in the groin, sent up into the brain and released to induce clotting. That's what I'd eventually learn. All I knew at the time was that the procedure was "minimally invasive." That meant nobody was going to shave all my hair off.

I was in intensive care for two weeks. On and off, I had spasms, called cerebral vasospasms, a result of the constricting of the blood vessels in the brain. The spasms felt like giant charley horses throughout my whole body. Mama visited once with Ricky. Ricky pushed her into the room in a wheelchair. She'd had a fall in a store somewhere and all she seemed to want to talk about was the lawsuit friends of hers were suggesting she file.

Back home, Nada was there for me when I first got out of the hospital. It took me another couple months to recover, dealing with the spasms all the while. It was difficult to even get around. During the time of my recovery, I had a place that could take care of a black lab mix I'd adopted named Sammy. He had a tuxedo fur pattern and I'd rescued him in 2012 when he was six months old. Sammy had become the best, most loyal companion I'd ever known. We went everywhere together. He was my Baskin-Robbins road partner, going with me to get ice cream and getting a puppy cup and enjoying himself a few licks. I had been taking Sammy, spoiled as ever, to daycare at PetSmart Doggie Day Camp practically every day and that's where he was when I'd been rushed to the hospital. They loved Sammy at the day camp and made arrangements to care for him until I was back home and on my feet. While I was in intensive care, Sammy was living it up in a dog hotel where, happily again, ice cream was served.

I lost Sammy a few short years afterward in April of 2019. He was only seven. He started slowing down and wasn't as feisty as he used to be. Normally, when I would grab the keys to my truck, he'd go straight to the door, ready to ride. Now, he barely sat up. Then he developed a cough and became even more sluggish. There was blood in his urine. I took him to the vet who said his heart was failing. He stopped eating. Four days later, I knew it was time. I was going to lose my baby. The vet came over to the house and we put Sammy to sleep. I knew Sammy was ready. I had him wrapped in my favorite blanket. It read: "All I want to do is drink my wine and pet my dog." I propped his head on his little pillow so that I could look into his eyes and whisper to him that I loved him before he went.

Word spread throughout the apartment complex. Sammy was well known. I had a corner apartment on the end. Everyone always passed our place and nobody could miss Sammy out on the patio. Neighbors dropped by that day and offered their condolences. The property's maintenance guys had gotten to know Sammy and they came by too. Stephanie came over. I kept telling myself I'd given Sammy the best life I could, and I prayed I was right. Of course Jerry and Ricky and Mama had known how close I was to Sammy, but I didn't hear a word from any of them.

Chapter 17

Trying to Move On

In March 2017, A couple of years after Daddy died, there was a fire at Mama's house, an electrical fire that started in the basement. Two young neighbor boys saw the smoke and pounded on Mama's door to alert her. She answered, but she had a security screen door in place that she kept locked. Mama kept the key in a little table by the door but in her confusion, she froze. The boys had to break a window to get her out of the house.

I got the news from an old friend I'd grown up within the neighborhood. Neither Ricky nor Jerry called me. By then, I think they realized I had more or less cut them out of my life for my own peace of mind. The house was seriously smoke-damaged and Jerry took Mama in. But his water heater was broken and he needed to leave her with someone for a few hours while it was getting fixed. Naturally, he thought of me.

He brought Mama over to my place. Nada was there. It was the day after the fire, but Mama still looked like she had just walked out of it. I got her cleaned up and then went to Family Dollar to buy her some underclothes and toiletries while Nada fixed her something to eat. When I got back, I gave Mama a bath, dressed her in some of my clothes, and we sat out on the patio. I showed her some pictures of my latest trip to Italy, but her mind was elsewhere. Out of the blue, she said, "You know, I just didn't notice the fire. I didn't even smell any smoke." Mama was in shock. Worse, I supposed by then that her mind was going. Was it shock that had caused her to freeze at the door, or was it dementia?

Either way, she needed a place to live. All I knew was that it wasn't going to be with me. I gave Jerry a courtesy call, reminding him, in case he'd forgotten, that Mama was still waiting on him. Finally, he came by and got her. A few days after that, he took Mama to a cheap Days Inn near the interstate, off of I-65 near a truck stop. Eventually, he moved her to a Marriott Residence Inn not far from me. I went to visit her and she wondered what was going to become of her. I had no answer. A friend she'd worked with at Kroger's for thirty years took her in for a while after that. Ultimately, my brothers made the decision to sell the house as is. With the sale proceeds and some insurance money, Mama had enough to go to an assisted living facility.

All this time, since Daddy's funeral, in fact, I had seen Mama as little as possible. She was still my mother. She always would be. But we never had anything to say. Ours was not a relationship of any substance. She'd always make it a point to tell me how much Jerry was doing for her, even though I knew Jerry wasn't doing a damn thing for her. Neither was Ricky. In fact, they'd never stopped trying to get me to do things for Mama. Word got to me that since I was the daughter, I should be the one caring for her. And of course, visiting Mama always meant there was a chance of running into Jerry or Ricky. I stayed away. When I did go, it was out of obligation. Just like it was out of obligation that Jerry and Ricky had gone to see Daddy, the few times they'd gone to see him. But I knew that Mama wasn't much more in their eyes than an obligation either.

The last time I saw Mama was in 2018. It was just before Thanksgiving and I visited her in the assisted living facility with Sammy, who was still alive and well at that time. I'd had him for six years and Mama liked him. Funny thing is, he couldn't stand Ricky. He'd growl menacingly whenever Ricky was around.

Dogs weren't allowed in Mama's building so I went in and took her outside. As she played with Sammy, I made idle conversation with her. Told her I was about to travel to Texas to visit Nada, but, as usual, there wasn't a lot that was said. I made a decision then that I was going to steer clear of Mama from there on out. It was a decision that had its roots out on my porch that day after the fire. I knew then that I could no longer invest myself emotionally in this woman. What we had was an empty shell of a mother-daughter relationship, and it had been a one-sided one since I was a girl. I'd been trying unsuccessfully to please Mama since the Kroger incident and before. I could never do enough. And I was tired of trying.

A little more than a year after that Thanksgiving, in December of 2019, Mama died. Tina's aunt Sheila called to offer her condolences. Instead, since once again neither Ricky nor Jerry called me, Aunt Sheila ended up breaking the news. "I can't believe it about Miss Mary," she said. "I was just talking with her the other day."

"What, is she dead?" I asked.

"You mean Ricky or Jerry didn't call you?" she said. "Oh, baby, I'm sorry. I thought you knew."

"It's okay," I told her.

When we hung up, I took stock of how I felt. It was relief. Some for me, but also some for Mama. For my part, I knew I'd never again have to feel guilty for not going to see her. For Mama's sake, I knew she hadn't been well. In fact, earlier that year, while I was traveling, Stephanie had called me to tell me she'd had a stroke.

Then I called a couple of my old Navy buddies who knew my story. They said pretty much the same thing, that I had done the best I could for her. After those calls, I broke down. But I knew they were tears of relief. What I was feeling was a sense of what I can only describe as being released from something. And it was a feeling I didn't want to lose. I cleared out of town. I didn't want to know anything about the funeral. I checked into the Belterra Casino Resort and Spa, where I'd often retreated, about an hour away in Indiana. I stayed there for three days, came back home, re-packed, then drove to Alabama to visit my nephew Keith. Then Houston to visit Nada. Then I came back home and got myself on a flight to Italy.

I returned in February of 2020 with my whole life now in front of me. There were no attachments any longer. Anyone who had meant anything to me in Louisville was gone—everyone who meant my heart good and everyone who meant my heart no good. The pressures were gone and I was ready to move away. I could go anywhere in the world and be whoever I wanted to be. Whoever *that* was. And for an extended length of time, if not for good.

And it was right about this time that I heard more disturbing news about some virus that I had first heard about while in Italy. The virus had started in

China. It was spreading throughout Asia and Europe. In fact, when I'd left Naples, it had been reported in Milan. By the time I got home, it was in Naples. Now there were a few cases in the United States. And then there were more cases. And then a lot more cases. People were dying. Sports leagues were shutting down. Businesses were closing down too. Travel bans went into effect. Some locations issued stay-at-home orders. By May, the death toll in the United States was over 100,000. And we were still months away from a vaccine.

Turned out, instead of beginning my new life of freedom, it looked like I wasn't going anywhere after all, at least not any time soon.

Chapter 18

Sailing Forth

I feel in some ways as if I breezed through the first couple of years of Covid. I put all of my coping resources into practice. And I began to write this book. The lockdowns and time spent alone gave me a rare opportunity for self-reflection. On the other hand, Covid 19 was a terrible scourge, producing death and disruption worldwide. Everyone was affected in one way or another. Everyone felt the anxiety and stress. And although no amount of stress should be taken lightly, it is a fact that people with underlying issues felt it more acutely. Like those of us with ADHD, for instance. Anxiety often accompanies our condition. So does depression. Regulating these negative feelings is an emotional roller-coaster. As mentioned, our brains have a tendency to become flooded with emotions that we cannot properly sort through.

And so in truth, the Covid years were bad. Of course, the virus hasn't gone away and may never go away, but the world seems to have reached survival mode. All of us have learned how to live with it—perhaps the best we can do. For me, the strain has been too much at times, but I try as best I can to break things down, take life a day at a time, and maintain my faith in God.

Which is to say that if you hoped for a nice, tidy ending to this book, complete with nifty and permanent solutions for the hardships wrought by ADHD, you might be disappointed. Then again, isn't this the case with life in general? Our lives—all of our lives—are works-in-progress, it seems to me. We never really reach a point where we have solutions to all our problems, until, of course, our very final day. Until then, we have to keep plugging, we have to keep our faith in whatever it is that gives us the courage and strength to move forward. To keep striving ahead, to reach for fulfillment and happiness—this, I believe, is what it means to be human whether we're living with ADHD, physical ailments, poverty, family problems, or whatever else it is that defines our lives.

Everybody's carrying something.

And that's okay. That's what it is to be alive. I've learned to take the bad with the good.

If you're living with ADHD and you *are* looking for some tangible advice, I would humbly submit that you could do worse than follow some of the suggestions within these pages, ideas that I have learned over the years. First of all, remember that ADHD is not a disease. "Disorder" isn't even appropriate. I like Hallowell and Ratey's term: VAST, Variable Attention Stimulus Trait. Remember, too, that, even if you consider it a disorder, as Barkley puts it, it's a disorder of *intention*, not *attention*. If anything, it's too much attention, more than can be properly managed. You can know stuff, Barkley says, but you won't do stuff. And it's not your fault. It's not a failure of will or strength; it's a physiological gap between parts of the brain.

In fact, far from being weak, people living with ADHD are, on balance, more resilient and more determined than the general population. I'd always assumed I had a certain sense of resiliency, but it wasn't until the writing of this book that I was able to see just what I'd accomplished in my career. It was shocking to me. I'd never given myself any credit, thinking of myself as scattered and disorganized and underachieving when the truth was otherwise. People living with ADHD can do extraordinary things. Even more so if the condition is properly managed.

Awareness, of course, is the first step. If anything you've read here resonates with you, please consider getting a definitive diagnosis. Find a doctor experienced with ADHD. The difference between me now and before I knew I had ADHD (or even knew what it is) is huge. I don't blame myself as much anymore. If I'm spiraling down with depression or suffering from anxiety, and I don't know why, I can remind myself that it's likely just the ADHD getting its licks in. I can better assess the moment and go from there. I can pull myself up before I spiral deeper.

Your doctor will tell you whether medication is appropriate. He or she might also recommend cognitive behavioral therapy, ACT—Acceptance and Commitment Therapy, or even a coach. Remember some of the workarounds, such as getting your thoughts out of the brain and putting them in external places like post-it notes and to-do lists. Practice time management. Remember Mahan's lifestyle advice on structure, good sleeping habits, proper diet, and meditation.

Finally, if you're not journaling, I'd like to suggest that you give it a try. Release your negative thoughts onto the written page. Forget any rules. Just get a line down. Then maybe another. I make it a point to journal every day. Anywhere I happen to be. And if I'm out somewhere and feel the need, I'm not too fussy about the form of stationery. I've journaled on napkins, menus, and programs.

Not long ago, I made a decision. I picked up on the idea I'd had before Covid hit. I decided to move, to get away and start a new life. All by myself. For my entire life, I had always had somebody or something to take care of. No more. I was done picking up strays. I was going to be my only stray. It was time for me to be whoever I wanted to be. I still wasn't sure who that was, but now that I could focus on myself for a change, I was ready to figure it out. It's a big world and Louisville wasn't feeling like home to me anymore. With Daddy and my Sammy gone, and even Mama, I could see no reason to stay.

I made a trip to the cemetery where Mama and Daddy are both buried. But not too close to each other. I told Daddy again how much I loved him and pulled the weeds from around his headstone. Then I found Mama's grave and did the same. I told her I was leaving. I told her that for her sake I was sorry I hadn't attended her funeral, but that for my sake, I wasn't sorry. I hope she understood. Either way, I'm confident that I've upheld the fifth commandment; I've honored my mother and father. I gave them both my entire life, each in very different ways.

Then I went back to my apartment, journaled a little, and then (still old-school) pulled out my road atlas of the United States. So many options. I thought of Europe too. Of course for a person with ADHD, having multiple options isn't always a good thing. But I'll break it down. I'll find my place. Somewhere near the ocean, no doubt, with my full armor of God.

I'll know when I get there.

And with resilience, patience, strength, and God's good grace, I'll keep sailing forth, with fair winds and following seas.

Epilogue

In the process of writing this book, I found myself surprised at times by my career accomplishments. It was almost as if I'd forgotten how far I'd made it. I never think of myself as a success story. Worse, on some level, I even question whether I have been deserving of my success. But in learning about ADHD, I learned why that is. Imposter syndrome is common for people living with ADHD. It goes hand in hand with our masking, our desire to fit in and conform to expectations. And our fears that we are not doing so.

Recently, I learned that I'm at triple risk for imposter syndrome. It turns out that it's experienced by women more than men, and by Black women more than white women. If you're Black, a woman, and have ADHD, you're almost destined to have imposter syndrome.

A big part of the reason, of course, is that women, and Black women in particular, are not traditionally thought of as wildly successful by the standards of American society. Women are underrepresented in positions of leadership, whether in the corporate world, in government, at universities, or in the military. Black women more so. Black women, in other words, are underrepresented among the underrepresented.

And so when we have the opportunity to advance, it's natural for us to feel as if we somehow don't belong. There aren't a lot of role models, after all. There aren't a lot of people in powerful positions that look like us. My mother worked her whole life for Kroger, in the checkout lane. I come from a lower working-class neighborhood in Louisville, Kentucky. I associate with that class. I relate to it. And it doesn't seem to matter that since I left Louisville as a young woman, I have been around the world, served in the US Navy for two decades, and achieved the rank of Chief Warrant Officer. In some sense, I still think of myself as that girl from Louisville, the one that got busted for shoplifting.

Part of this is Mama, of course. Part is society. But part is also the fact that I don't spend enough time giving myself the credit I deserve. And I know there are plenty of other people out there—Black, white, women, men, ADHD or no ADHD—who make the same mistake. If this is resonating with you, then you might be one of them. You may downgrade yourself unintentionally too. Like me, you probably don't acknowledge your successes.

As I put the finishing touches on this book, a new year is beginning. And I'm going to make it a point to start giving myself some of that credit I'm due. I'm going to start being kinder to myself. I hope you'll do the same.

Mama, a real piece of eye candy back in the day.

Daddy: handsome John Wesley "Jayhawk" Rucker.

My grandmother, "Mother" or "Muh" to us kids.
My rock.

Future Chief Warrant Officer.

My home growing up, in the Shawnee neighborhood of Louisville, Kentucky.

With Jay.

Me and Nada.

Still friends.

Me with a World War II vet at the Women in Military Service Memorial.

My ship. The *LaSalle*.

Moored in Gaeta, Italy.

With Gaeta behind me. Love that place.

With Mama at my commissioning ceremony.

Having a lollipop with Daddy.

Sammy, the sweetest companion.

Resources and Suggestions for Further Reading

Some of the people and resources mentioned in this book that have helped me tremendously:

Dr. Russell Barkley: russellbarkley.org
René Brooks: blackgirllostkeys.com
Dr. Edward Hallowell: drhallowell.com
Ryan Holiday: ryanholiday.net
Brendan Mahan: adhdessentials.com
Dr. J. Russell Ramsay: cbt4adhd.com
Dr. John Ratey: johnratey.com
ADDitude Magazine: additudemag.com
Understood For All, Inc.: understood.org

The Artist's Way, Julia Cameron, TarcherPerigee.

Cognitive Behavioral Therapy for Adult ADHD: Targeting Executive Dysfunction, Dr. Mary Solanto. The Guilford Press.

Mastering Your Adult ADHD: A Cognitive Behavioral Treatment Program, Safren, Sprich, Perlman, Otto. Oxford University Press.

Acknowledgments

My gratitude to those who have, over the years, suggested I write a book. Well, I finally did so. Thank you.

Thanks to my editor, Jerry Payne, for his encouragement, ability to keep me focused, and for helping me get the words right.

A shoutout to Robin and Stella Mountain of Ntaba Coffee Haus in Louisville for allowing me to spend my mornings and sometimes days working on my book in their wonderful establishment.

Above all, thank you Dear God for carrying me through all of my obstacles and successes with your never-ending grace and mercy. I love you.

Milton Keynes UK
Ingram Content Group UK Ltd.
UKHW022011040923
428063UK00005B/167

9 798988 184126